THE 1917 SPRING OFFENSIVES

Arras, Vimy, le Chemin des Dames

Written by Yves BUFFETAUT

Translated by Bernard Leprêtre

HISTOIRE & COLLECTIONS

Arras, April 1917

From Joffre's plan to the Ge

I N the late autumn of 1916, the Allies had not managed, in spite of their massive attack on the Somme, to break the German front anywhere. On the other hand, they had never been in such favourable position since the war had begun. True, 1916 was another year of huge slaughters. But the losses were distributed more fairly, if one may say so, than in the previous years. Even with the battles of Verdun and the Somme, the French army lost fewer men than in 1915 and especially 1914, as Britain now had, for the first time, a real army capable of sustaining a long and difficult campaign. Of course a better distribution of the war effort was an improvement, but it was not an end in itself, and the cumulated losses of both armies are astounding by 1997 standards. History, however, should not be judged with the criteria of later periods.

On 15 November 1916 general Joffre chaired a conference at Chantilly. Also attending were general Haig, the commander of the BEF, and representatives of the other allied countries. British official records describe the atmosphere as soberly optimistic. General Joffre was feeling justifiably confident, as in October the French army had recaptured the fort of Douaumont from the Germans in one day, thereby taking back most of the ground it had lost during the terrible months of the enemy offensive; moreover the British were pursuing their advance methodically along the Ancre valley and exhausting the reserves of the German army. While the Allies were well aware that they were inflicting enormous losses on their opponents, they probably did not fully realize their extent. German official records, however, leave no doubt on this point: 1,400,000 men were either killed, wounded or missing between January and October 1916, of whom 600,000 on the Somme alone, which was more than the combined British and French losses. Clearly, many of the wounded would be able to fight again sooner or later, but the depletion was all the more serious as Germany did not have unlimited reserves of men.

On 15 November 1916, the Allies were obviously superior in numbers on all fronts. On the western front, the one we are dealing with, this was unquestionable:

- Germany: 129 divisions;   ● Allies: 168 divisions
    The breakdown of allied divisions was:
- France: 107
- Great Britain: 56
- Belgium: 6

In Chantilly, the Allies decided to use their superiority and pursue their effort. Joffre wrote in his war diary that three principles had been set, the first two of which concerned the western front: "– *maintaining an offensive activity on the different fronts throughout the winter, together with preparing for offensives in the spring of 1917; – coordinating the offensives at the time within a period of three weeks, at a date to be agreed on by the commanders-in-chief, if possible in the first week of February*". It then appears clearly that Joffre, who enjoyed Haig's complete support – a significant fact in the absence of a unified command – did not want to give the Germans time to recover. Official British history on the two day's conference at Chantilly reached a conclusion which may even surprise us: "*It is not fanciful to think that if the gradual defection of Russia could have been avoided, as well as the instigator, the Great War would have ended in 1917*". The official point of view of the British army was thus that Joffre could have won the war in 1917, had he not been replaced by Nivelle after a political slandering campaign. The change in Commanders-in-Chief of the French armies is an essential element to understand the offensives or the spring of 1917.

The dismissal of Joffre was undoubtedly based on objective facts that will be examined later. But it was also brought about by vague theories that were then in favour, including a belief that only new men and new methods would be able to bring the country out of a war that

was bleeding it to death. The idea was in fashion in Britain as well as in France. In London, it was directed at the politicians and was certainly instrumental in Asquith's downfall and his subsequent replacement by Lloyd-George. In France, politicians managed to divert the criticisms towards the Grand Quartier Général, which actually wielded considerable power. As the war dragged on, Joffre came under increasing attacks. He was blamed for everything, from the lack of readiness at Verdun when the Germans attacked to the very heavy losses incurred on the Somme for minimal results, and even to Romania's fall at the end of 1916. His self-control and composure, which had been praised during the battle of the Marne, were now reviled, for it was commonly agreed that he was feeling comfortable in a war which had become a normal way of life for him. His very wish to see the British army take a bigger part in operations was considered as a sign of helplessness or of his lack of confidence in the French army. Furthermore, political men resented him for heeding only the advice of President Poincaré, président du conseil Aristide

Briand and the war minister, and ignoring all other members of the parlement and elected officials.

From June 1916, the parlement engaged in a tug-of-war with the government for the replacement of Joffre. Aristide Briand was not favourable to his dismissal, as he knew the remarkable coordination among Allies to be the work of Joffre and nobody else. During the battle of the Somme he managed to delay the changes in the GQG that were demanded by the parlement, but in December he resigned and the president gave him the task of forming a new cabinet. He appointed general Lyautey as war minister, and simulteneously created a war committee, headed by Poincaré, in which general Joffre acted as a "technical adviser" while retaining his position as commander-in-chief of the French armies. However this deprived him of the real control on the most important front, as at the same time general Nivelle became the commander-in-chief of the armées du Nord et du

Nord-Est. Joffre agreed to this change in his role because he had obtained that Nivelle in France and Sarrail in Macedonia be placed under his direct orders. But on 21 December, the *Parlement* obtained that Nivelle should receive his orders directly from the government and might deal with the British and Belgian armies without reporting to Joffre. This was of course not acceptable for the commander-in-chief of French armies, who was in effect losing all real control. On 25 December Joffre tendered his resignation, which was accepted. On the same day president Poincaré elevated him to the rank of *Maréchal de France*, thereby reviving a long-forgotten dignity. Nivelle was not given the rank of commander-in-chief of French armies but neverthe-less was the sole commander. Nivelle was far from young when he arrived at this position; he had just turned 60, whereas "old" Joffre was 65. Still a colonel in the artillery in 1914, his career had been indifferent in peacetime, but it had become dazzling since the begin-ning of the war. His appointment at the very top job was al the more remarkable as in December 1916 he had only recently become a

Général d'armée and was thus passing ahead of four other *Commandants de groupes d'armées*: Foch, Pétain, Franchet d'Espérey and de Castelnau.

Nivelle seems to owe his commission as commander-in-chief of the French armies largely to the attack of 24 October 1916 against the fort of Douaumont. Led by general Mangin and supported by impressive artillery fire, the assault had been a complete success. Nivelle had shown that in a matter of hours French troops had been able to capture a powerfully defended terrain that the Germans had conquered after eight months of gruesome sacrifice. On 15 December 1916, he achieved a similar feat by recapturing the second French line that had been lost on 24 February. On a six-mile wide, two-mile deep front, four French divisions had broken through five German divisions in one day, taking 11,000 prisoners and reaching all their targets but one, Bezonvaux, that fell the next morning.

These two remarkable achievements led general Nivelle to think that he could renew them wherever he chose. It has often been said, after Nivelle's disgrace, that his theory was merely copied from the all-too famous Grandmaison school of thought which had been responsible for the terrible slaughters of 1914. This is a gross misrepresentation. Nivelle was, first and foremost, an artillery man. He had understood that the infantry was powerless by itself, but that the artillery, if used intelligently, could prepare the ground. His theory was that, by des-troying the enemy's defenses with a bombardment of unprecedented force, followed with an artillery barrage of unprecedented depth, he was confident he could in one day capture the whole German system as deep down as the battery line. Accordingly he thought that, with an unsuspected and mighty strike taking advantage of the enemy's sur-prise, and if he selected a point in the front that was not too strongly defended, he could resume mobile warfare.

To him success made no doubt, like a mathematical proposition, and this is definitely where he went wrong. Nivelle seemed to be strongly influenced by colonel d'Alenson, his chief adviser, who had an even deeper faith in the solidity of the theory.

Whatever Nivelle's intellectual qualities may have been, not every-body - and particularly Britain was pleased by Joffre being put aside. Haig himself tried to convince Briand of the danger of replacing Joffre. British official records conclude: *"Only when he was no longer there did the Allies in general realize how much good sense had emanated from him"*.

Joffre's good sense was replaced by Nivelle's inspiration. He planned an offensive as early as February 1917, on three different points of the front, with a British assault between Arras and Bapaume, and two French assaults, one north of the Oise, the second between Soissons and Rheims. The latter, at Chemin des Dames, was regarded as the key battle. There was a considerable difference between Joffre and Nivelle's conceptions: whereas the former thought he could bring down the enemy's resistance by wearing them out in an offensive similar to the Somme's, Nivelle thought he would destroy their reserves in a mobile warfare battle. In order to do this, however, he had to break up the front first.

We will not dwell here upon the difficult relationship between Haig and Nivelle, which go well beyond the scope of this book. It soon became evident that February 1917 was much too early a date for a vast offensive. And before this could be launched, a major event changed the whole aspect of the western front: on 25 February 1917, the Germans began a withdrawal movement that had no precedent in size. This rendered the allied preparations in Artois and north of the Oise completely useless, as the Germans withdrew almost 25 miles back, giving up the towns of Bapaume, Péronne, Roye, Ham, Noyon and Chauny. It came as a total surprise for both Haig and Nivelle.

▲

General Joffre is inspecting troops
of the 4e régiment colonial

The scene is at Chantilly, where the GQG was installed, not in the famous chateau as legend would have it, but at the Hôtel du Grand Condé.
(BDIC/Archipel)

A strange German movement

A German ambulance is retreating at Ecquancourt, March 1917. ►

Because of their losses in Verdun and on the Somme, the Germans were no longer capable of holding an extended front. Also, Ludendorff wanted to constitute a strategic reserve that could be sent wherever danger was greatest.
As Germany no longer had any human reserves, it was necessary to take divisions where they could be found, that is at the front. A shorter front meant a deep withdrawal to a defensive position, the Siegfried Stellung, called the Hindenburg line by the Allies, that stretched from the vicinity of Arras to Lavaux, at the western end of Chemin des Dames. The retreat was to be known as Operation *Alberich*. It was carried out under the orders of Kronprinz of Bavaria Rupprecht, who was in command of the group of armies in the area.
(Bundesarchiv)

Civilians are being evacuated during the Alberich movement.

As they withdrew, the Germans decided to turn the area they were leaving into wasteland in order to hamper the Allies' movements in their expected pursuit. Moreover, most of the population was transported eastwards, to cut off the Allies' possible supply of men for work or armed service. Those who couldn't work, on the other hand, were left in towns such as Noyon, Ham or Nesle with a few days' food supplies. This exodus took place in terrible conditions, the winter of 1916-1917 being the most severe of the war. ▼
(Bundesarchiv)

Women left behind in
Nesle by the Germans
talking to French
and British soldiers.

The town of Nesle, close to Roye,
was at the junction of the British
and French lines. The German
withdrawal was a complete
surprise for the Allies, even
though they knew of the existence
of the Siegfried line. The signs of
a German withdrawal were first
reported by the British troops
on the Somme battlefield.
On 22 February, a patrol led
by lieutenant Lucas of
the 7/R. West Kent found that
the German outposts in the
Petit Miraumont sector had
been deserted.
(IWM)

While retreating,
the Germans cut
down all fruit trees. ▶

Considered by the French as
pure vandalism, the destruction
of the country's resources was
indeed contrary to The Hague
convention.
(IWM)

March 1917. Men of the
Notts and Derby Regiment
are moving along the road from
Amiens to Saint-Quentin, in Brie.

The orchard in the background
has been completely destroyed
by the Germans. The British
soldiers are befriending the
children by giving them rides
on their bicycles. The civilian
population is solely made up of
women and children that the
Germans did not want to have
to feed if they took them east.
By 25 February, the evidence of a
German retreat made little doubt,
but on the same day the 2nd
Australian Division, who wanted
to follow close on the Germans'
heels, was held back by serious
enemy machine-gun fire near
Warlencourt. It then became clear
that the pursuit would be no easy
task, even though the men were
eager to engage the Germans,
certain as they were that if they
could surprise them on open
ground, far from the havoc of the
battlefield, they could beat them.
(IWM)

A country laid to waste

March 1917,
in Bovincourt.
The British army's official
photographer's car is
bringing food to civilians.

Chasing the German
army was made even
more difficult by the road
conditions on both sides
of the former front,
particularly in the British
sector where traffic soon
became impossible except
for the lighter or horse-
drawn vehicles.
(IWM)

A picture of the German retreat: a medical detachment on the streets of Cagnicourt. ▲

The withdrawal of Kronprinz Rupprecht's troops was a success, though one may hardly agree with Ludendorff's description of it as a brilliant feat. A clear confession of weakness from the German high command, it was allayed by the consequences of operation Alberich. Ludendorff summed them up in these words: "*This shortening of our front made it stronger and safer. The enemy's plans were countered. The lines of attack they had chosen were no longer suitable and the ground we had abandoned left them no resources. If they wanted to use it, they had to repair everything and very heavy work was necessary in* order to prepare an attack. As a consequence the enemy came to face our new front with relatively reduced numbers. We could accordingly, on our side, thin out the troops and withdraw divisions. The result that had been sought by operation Alberich and the occupation of the Siegfried position was fully reached*".
(BA)

◄ April 1917 in Athies. British troops are walking past the demolished church.

The Germans destroyed everything that could be of any use to the Allies over a ten-mile deep area before the Siegfried Stellung. Thus the church steeples, that could be used as observation posts, were blown up. All trees close to roads were cut down. Ludendorff described the retreating manoeuvre in his memoirs: "*The main point was to avoid a battle. We also had to salvage all the equipment that was not built into the ground and the raw materials necessary to warfare, to destroy communication lines, villages and wells, in order to prevent a massive and quick occupation of the terrain by the enemy. The order was issued that springs were not to be poisoned*".
(IWM)

A Royal Engineers
party on the outskirts of Arras. ▶

Over all the area of the front
left by the Germans, the Allies
had to start major works to
repair the roads and villages
that had been systematically
destroyed. Any idea of an
offensive launched from the
recently liberated zone had to
be forgotten, which reduced
the possible assault area.
(IWM)

The German withdrawal was a nuisance to the Allies

Extensive destruction
in the village of Athies.

A huge crater sits in the
middle of the main street and
prevents all road traffic.
The French press and public
opinion loosed their fury
on German vandalism.
(IWM) ▼

March 1917 in Frize.
A water detail of French and British soldiers around a well. ▲

The Allies' surprise at the German withdrawal was such that the French GQG simply denied its reality until mid-March. While there was evidence of the enemy's retreat on the British front, where English troops remained on the offensive throughout winter, the French high command could not bring itself to believe that the Germans were withdrawing of their own accord, a sign that they no longer hoped to defeat the French army. In addition, the unexpected retreat thwarted the GQG's plans. The French spent several weeks waiting. *(IWM)*

◄ A street in Bapaume as found by the Australians on the day of the town's capture, 17 March 1917.

Bapaume was one of the targets of the previous summer's Somme offensive, and there is no doubt that the exhaustion of the German army on the Somme was the original reason behind operation Alberich. The town had just been abandoned by the Germans. Many houses were still on fire. The destructions in Bapaume looked worse than anywhere else, to the possible exception of Péronne. However, when the Australians discovered intact landscapes just behind the town, free from shell holes and bomb craters, they experienced an amazing sense of victory. Could the Germans want to stop? Was a war of movement possible again? *(IWM)*

Map of the German retreat.

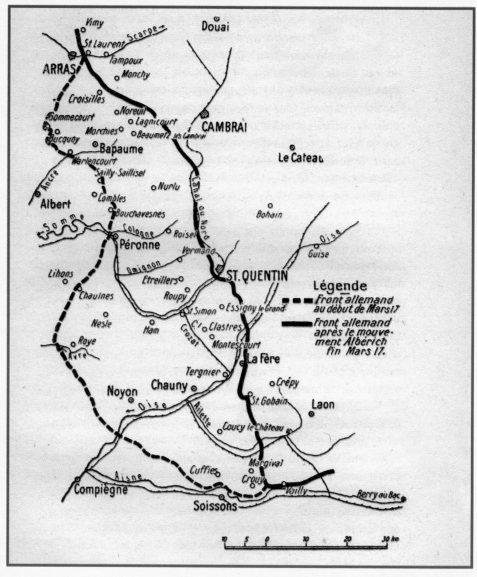

Jean de Panafieu, who wrote the GQG's daily communiqué, left a remarkable description of the response of Nivelle's staff to the enemy retreat: *"Consternation was the word at the general's headquarters; everyone looked grim. The offensive that had been so carefully prepared was falling through. Nevertheless, enough self-control was regained to take advantage of the situation. (...). I was given the task of making the communiqués read as if the enemy had withdrawn under our relentless pressure and we were energetically pursuing them, driving their rearguard off the field and constantly on their heels. (...). The staff was haunted by the desire not to betray the fact that they had been surprised and I believe that no one on earth could have made the general confess that, until March 15, he had miscalculated the Germans' intentions"*.

Légende
- - - - *Front allemand au début de Mars 17*
——— *Front allemand après le mouvement Albérich fin Mars 17.*

The offensive falls through

A view of the destructions in Bapaume ▲
at the time of the town's liberation.

**The snapshot was taken by a photographer
of the 1st Anzac Corps from the town hall
belfry on 19 March 1917.** *(IWM)*

▼ 19 March 1917 in Bapaume.

**Men of the 30th Battalion,
Australian Imperial Forces, are
posing with various trophies
in the ruins of the town.** *(IWM)*

◄ *Previous page,
a patrol of the 2nd Australian
Division in rue de Péronne,
Bapaume, on March 19 1917.*

**The town had then been under
allied control for two days. The
photograph gives a good idea of
the condition the Germans had
left the town in: to the exception
of horses and men on foot, no
one could use the streets. Also,
traps were everywhere. On the
evening of March 18, general
Gough decided, to engage the
cavalry to push the Germans as
far back as possible towards the
Hindenburg line. In spite of some
machine-gun fire, the Australians
and Lucknow's cavalry brigade
made a considerable advance
on the 19th, past Bapaume
and into the villages of Vélu and
Lebucquière. However all
attempts at encircling the
retreating enemy failed:
the 21st and 23rd Australian
Battalions were vigorously held
back near the Siegfried Stellung
and lost 331 men for meagre
results. It then became clear
that nothing would be possible
without a strong artillery support.**
(IWM)

Previous page, an Australian soldier is engraving his name on a pedestal facing the town hall of Bapaume.

Many others imitated him in the few days following the liberation of the town. Gingerly perched on top of the pedestal is a stove pipe meant to represent an AA gun. Seen from a high altitude, the resemblance must have been reasonably good. The town hall is seen in the background, still intact then as it had been time-mined and was to explode at the very moment of the French civilian authorities' arrival, causing many casualties. *(IWM)*

A view of the Grand-Place in Arras.

The historic house fronts have collapsed under artillery fire. Only the inside remains, sometimes intact. *(IWM)*

The ruins of the city hall in Arras are as impressive as hose of the Cloth Hall in Ypres.

In spite of the city's extensive destructions, the Allied attempted to liberate it during their spring offensive. *(IWM)*

 The ruins in Arras just before the allied offensive.

The administrative centre of the département of Pas-de-Calais had remained within allied territory since 1914, but the proximity of the front, a few thousands of yards away, accounts for the condition of the two main squares. The city hall, considered by the Germans as an observation post, suffered most. *(IWM)*

The British plan and available strengths

EVEN though the allied command was not unified, it goes without saying that general Nivelle and general Haig were constantly working together on the preparation of a common offensive on the western front. As the British attack preceded the French one by a week, it seems logical to start with the former.

Early in the year 1917, Nivelle informed Haig that he was thinking of a threefold attack on the German positions: a preliminary French assault between the Oise and Avre rivers, a powerful British offensive between Bapaume and Arras and finally the main push of the French army between Rheims and Vailly, on the Aisne, that is to say at Chemin des Dames.

The German retreat had made the French plans for an attack between the Oise and Avre obsolete. Furthermore it obliged the British to shift the main line of their attack further north. The chief French offensive, on the other hand, was not affected. This meant that, from the vicinity of Arras to the banks of the Aisne, the Allies were in no position to lead a powerful attack against a front that was over sixty miles wide: a definite achievement of the Alberich manoeuvre.

However, the terrain on which the British were to fight was by no means unfavourable: the Artois plateau was flat and obstacles were few and far between, apart from the Scarpe, which flowed west and did not have to be crossed. The openfield landscape was free from woods, with only a few clumps of trees and the occasional hedge. There were few hills, with the exception of a hillock at Monchy-le-Preux, which gave a commanding view of the area between Arras to the west and Cambrai to the east. This was in the German lines. North of the Scarpe, the land was much more hilly, with the Vimy ridge as its main feature. But it was steep on the German side only, where it overlooked the plain of Douai by two hundred feet. Its chalky soil was flaky and quickly turned into a limy mud. The last important element in the geography of the area was the city of Arras, just over a mile from the first lines. Though heavily shelled, it was still of value to British troops, as most roads converged there. Moreover it supplied a perfect screen for troop movements. The houses may have offered a dangerous kind of shelter, but the city was crisscrossed by numerous underground galleries, caves and quaries that were so many perfectly safe shelters.

On the other side were rather formidable German defenses. The labyrinth-like first line was made up of three or four trenches, 80 to 160 yards from each other, linked by connecting trenches every hundred yards. About half a mile behind this was the support line, the actual Siegfried Stellung, or Hindenburg line as it was known to the British. This was a very deep reserve line, often doubled and in places reinforced by genuine strongholds, such as the one close to the Feuchy chapel, on the road from Arras to Cambrai. The British often referred to this as the Wancourt-Feuchy line (or Point du Jour line north of the Scarpe). Finally, some four miles back, was the last line of defense, of which the British formed only a vague idea and that they were later to call the Drocourt-Quéant Switch. In the coming battle, the German lines were given British designations which it is best to know:
- Black line: first line;
- Blue line: support positions;
- Brown line: Wancourt-Feuchy line.

The British plan was simple out of necessity, as the trench war made any attempt at encirclement impossible as long as the enemy's defense positions had not been captured and the front broken through. The date for the attack was known as Z day, to be preceded by four days of massive artillery fire called V, W, X and Y. The Third Army was to attack in front of Arras with three corps, namely, going from right to left, VII., VI. and XVII., between Croisilles and Commander's House, a building that stood southwest of the Farbus wood. Their target was to capture the Hindenburg line and move on towards Cambrai.

To the north, the First Army was to attack from Givenchy-en-Gohelle to Commander's House, with the Vimy ridge as its main objective. Finally, at a later date, the Fifth Army would engage the Hindenburg line in the Bullecourt sector, south of the Third Army's front.

As the hope of capturing the Hindenburg line was very real, Haig had planned for the cavalry to be close enough to the front for a quick intervention in case the enemy lines were broken. As a consequence the 2nd and 3rd Cavalry Divisions were placed under the command of the Third Army, while the 4th Cavalry Division was under the orders of general Gough, the commander of the 5th Army. Finally the 1st Cavalry Division, under direct GHQ orders, was left to attack in any sector where the need or opportunity might arise.

A reserve of three divisions made up XVIII. Corps, in the Third Army's area, so that the latter was constituted of five corps including the Cavalry Corps, for a total of 16 divisions - an impressive strength, all the more as two divisions waiting further back were able to be on the field within 48 hours. Another chapter will deal with the preparations and available strengths of the First Army facing the Vimy ridge.

From north to south, the Third Army had the following divisions ready for the Z day attack:
- XVIII. Corps: 51st (Highland), 34th and 9th (Scottish) Divisions;
- VI. Corps: 15th (Scottish), 12th (Eastern) and 3rd Divisions;
- VII. Corps: 14th (Light), 56th (1st London), 30th and 21st Divisions.

The proportion of Scottish troops was high, as 44 out of the 120 battalions of the 10 attack divisions were from Scotland. There was also a South African brigade, with all the other battalions being English. In the north, the First Army included several Canadian divisions, while in the south the Fifth Army included the chiefly Australian I Anzac Corps.

On the German side, several divisions were relieved just before the British assault, so that four of the five divisions facing the Third Army were fresh. They were, from north to south:
- 1. Bayerische Reserve Division (a very good division);
- 14. Bayerische Division (a very good division);
- 11. Infanterie Division (a good division);
- 17. Reserve Infanterie Division (fair);
- 18. Reserve Infanterie Division (fair).

These five divisions were accordingly above average, and the two Bavarian divisions were even feared by the British, who found Bavarian troops superior to almost any other German units. It will be seen later that in additon to these first line divisions, the Germans had reserves ready to move in at fairly short notice.

A 9.2-inch (230-mm) piece of ordnance of the 91st Battery, Royal Garrison Artillery, ready for action in front of Arras, on April 1st, 1917. ►

The main difference between the battles of Arras and the Somme was the strong reinforcement of British artillery, mainly in heavy guns and ammunition stock. There were 92 230-mm howitzers of this type on the Third Army's front alone. All together, from the 858 18-pdr guns to the five 380-mm howitzers, the British had one gun every forty feet. *(IWM)*

Army artillery

Two 6-inch (150-mm) Mk VII guns on the streets of Albert, February 1917.

For his Arras offensive, general Allenby had 24 guns and 220 howitzers of the same calibre. The howitzers were given the task of destroying enemy trenches and shelters, while the cannons, which had a longer range, were preferably affected to counter-battery missions in order to silence the enemy artillery.
(IWM)

Moving around heavy ordnance near the front was no easy task.

Under the impressive span of a 150-mm gun, a John Fowler steam tractor has got stuck in the mud. This unit, like all heavy guns, belonged to the Royal Garrison Artillery, while the lighter pieces belonged to the Royal Field Artillery or the Royal Horse Artillery, in cavalry divisions. The use of artillery had been more carefully planned than on the Somme: although they had large ammunition stocks, gunners had been instructed not to try to destroy all enemy positions by indiscriminate fire.
(IWM)

A 9.2-inch howitzer in action among the ruins of Tilloy-les-Mofflaines, May 1917.

As is shown by both the date and location, this howitzer was photographed after the Arras offensive was launched on Easter Monday, the 9th of April. Before this, Tilloy-les-Mofflaines was right in the middle of the Hindenburg line, just south of the Arras-Cambrai road. This type of howitzer was used for counter-battery fire and the destruction of distant targets.
(IWM)

April 1917, near Arras. A 12-inch (300-mm) gun on railway.

The artillery on railway was not as common in the British as in the French Army. The former only lined up two in the battle of Arras. Indeed such powerful guns were extremely costly and went first to the Royal Navy. The two 12-inch guns and the 9.2-inch guns were assigned for use against selected targets, namely regiments' headquarters at the hill of Monchy-le-Preux, railway junctions, and so on. As far as possible, fire was directed by observation and artillery cooperation aircraft.
(IWM)

A 15-inch (380 mm)
howitzer ready to fire. ▲

The gunners are proudly posing
for the photographer. The five
howitzers of this type had been
assigned the task of bombarding
far-away villages and the enemy
batteries that might be placed
there, as well as bridges. The
use of artillery had been perfectly
prepared thanks to the lessons
learnt during the Somme
campaign in 1916.
(IWM)

British ordnance
in action

An 18-pdr piece
is being unlimbered. ▶

(IWM)

A battery of
five 60-pdr guns in
the battle of Arras. ▶

The aspect of the terrain
and the absence of any kind
of shelter give evidence
that this picture was taken
during the British advance,
after April 9. Over all their
front of attack, the Third Army,
the Canadian Corps at Vimy
and those units of the First Army
that were to join the offensive
later had 258 guns of this
type. They were used to shell
German quarters, narrow-gauge
railway lines, communication
trenches, etc.
(IWM)

A battery of 4.5-inch
(112-mm) howitzers
in the eastern suburbs of Arras. ▶

**These guns were given the task
of supporting the 18-pdr guns
against the enemy wire and
helping in the destruction of the
second and third German lines.
There were as many as 276 of
these howitzers in the Third
Army. This was the most common
type, the equivalent to the French
75 and the German 77. It will be
noticed that the houses in the
background are all intact, in
strange contrast with the ruins
seen on the photographs of the
city's famous two squares at the
same time: the Germans had
concentrated their fire on the
central part of the city, probably
in the hope of bringing down the
city hall belfry.**
(IWM)

On 12 April 1917,
an 18-pdr cannon is being
deployed in a graveyard in Arras.

**The 18-pdr guns had received
the all-important task of
destroying the enemy's wire,
mainly in the second and third
lines, as the remainder were
within range of the 2-inch
(50 mm) trench mortars.
The Third Army had
858 18-pdr pieces.**
(IWM)

▼

The artillery's task

The British Army, like all other armies at the time, still made extensive use of horse-drawn vehicles, but engine-powered vehicles were multiplying. They transported mainly ammunition, an area in which the British had made considerable efforts. Indeed, over the three months prior to the battle of the Somme, Haig had received 706,222 shells of all calibres. In the last three months of 1916, the number rose to 2,841,555. And during the second term of 1917, in which were fought the battles of Arras and Messines, it reached more than 5,000,000.
(IWM)

A battery of 4.5-inch howitzers
in the public park of Arras, 4 April.

Along with artillery preparation fire, all aspects of which have just been dealt with according to the various calibres, an essential role of the artillery was barrage fire to support the infantry. To this end, the 4.5-inch guns were assigned the German lines' support trenches as a fixed target, while the 18-pdrs' creeping fire was to move along with the infantry's advance.

This was made up of half explosive shells and half shrapnel shells. When the creeping fire met with the fixed barrage, the 4.5-inch howitzers were to aim at the next target. Meanwhile, a number of 60-pdr's were seeking possible resistance spots behind the front to shell and destroy them. Last of all, the heavy guns were in charge of counter-battery fire, blinding enemy observation positions and destroying telephone lines. *(IWM)*

▼

The Third Army's forty tanks

Lusitania and Iron Duke, ▶
two of the tanks of
 colonel Carr's 1st Brigade.

The 1st Brigade was then
known as the Heavy Branch
or Heavy Section, Machine Gun
Corps. Eight of the tanks had
been assigned to XVII. Corps
and sixteen to each
of the other two corps.
The tanks - modified Mark Is,
or Mark IIs - were not wholly
reliable, however the Mark IVs
were not available yet.
The tanks were not engaged
against the German first line,
reputedly an easy target for
the infantry, but against the
next lines that were much more
strongly defended and difficult to
capture. The main objective, the
chapel at Feuchy, was attacked
by eighteen tanks: it was a real
stronghold.
(IWM)

◀ British Engineers on the banks of the Scarpe.

The layout of the battlefield at Arras was such that the Third and First armies were seperated by the Scarpe, flowing at a right angle to the front and parallel to the lines of attack. On this picture, the row barge used to cross over is probably not as interesting a feature as the railway track running along the river, on the left. Numerous trains were needed to supply the artillery with ammunition. For instance, an 18-pdr could fire up to 300 shells in 24 hours. As there were 858 such guns in the Third Army, they needed more than 254,000 shells every day! This shows how vital the Engineers' work was to the success of the British operation.
(IWM)

▼

British cavalrymen waiting
to be called into battle, close
to the Arras to Cambrai road.

The men are partly sheltered
in a shallow dug-out. The horse
standing on the right has an
unuusal harness, the use of
which is not clear. It can be
inferred from the space taken
up by the small cases and the
lack of stirrups that it had no
rider. The cavalry was supposed
to be called in after the Brown
Line had been broken through.
(IWM)

The role of the cavalry

A partial view of a cavalry
division camp on the road
from Saint-Pol-sur-Ternoise to
Arras, just before the offensive.

The original caption gives no
further details, but this is enough
to identify the unit: only one
cavalry division was on that
road on April 9 1917, the First
Cavalry Division, a reserve of
GHQ. Should the Brown Line
be crossed by the infantry, the
cavalry was then to move up to
the Green Line, literally on the
infantry's heels, so as to take

advantage of the breaking of the
front with no time lost. Any delay
would allow the Germans to rally.
The cavalry's target on open
terrain was to reach the left bank
of the Sensée between Chérisy
and Vis-en-Artois, then on to
Boiry-Notre-Dame, between
Cambrai and Douai, so that the
enemy would not know where to
expect the next attack to move to.
(IWM)

Indian cavalrymen
of the 9th Hodson's Horse,
near Vraignes, April 1917.

The Cavalry Corps included five
divisions in 1917. On 25 November
1916, the 1st and 2nd Indian Cavalry
Divisions were renamed 4th and
5th Cavalry Divisions. The 4th Division
was placed under general Gough's
orders for his future attack
on Bullecourt. *(IWM)*

Men of the City of London Regiment are sitting in front of superbly built shelters.

The Arras region was rich in underground caves and galleries, which gave the infantry a perfect shelter, sometimes less than a thousand yards from the first line. The Saint-Sauveur tunnel, for instance, could accomodate 2,000, and the Christchurch cave over 4,000. The basements under Arras' two central squares hosted 13,000 men.
(IWM)

The infantry on the day before the assault

Wood ladders are being put up in the trenches on the day before the assault, Easter Sunday, 8 April 1917.

Ten divisions were to attack on the next day, and many such ladders were needed. They had to be strong, too, as the basic infantryman was heavily loaded: in addition to his rifle, his bayonet, his trench tool, a full flask, a piece of waterproof cloth and a haversack with two days' rations and other necessities, he had to take along 170 cartridges, two Mills grenades and three sand bags - empty. Moreover some men went into the attack with a spade or a pickaxe, not to bash in the enemies' skulls but for faster shelter digging. Wire cutters were also indispensable. ▶
(IWM)

Cheering British infantry on board commandeered double-deckers.

As is shown by these men back from the capture of Monchy-le-Preux, British morale was at its highest in April 1917, just as it was in French ranks on the day before the offensive.
(IWM)

An English soldier is confident enough to take a nap on a bed of enemy shells. ▶

This kind of morale was lacking in many German soldiers: the retreat, though a tactical success, had still left a bitter taste for most German fighters, as had the hell-inspired memories of Verdun and the Somme.
(IWM)

A Be 2e of the Royal Flying ► Corps in 1917.

This aircraft was definitely outclassed at the time of the Arras offensive. A reconnaissance and artillery cooperation plane, it was used in 19 squadrons on the western front. It was slow, and a sitting target for German hunters. *(MAP)*

British and German Air Forces

A British Fe 2b just after ▼ its capture by the Germans.

This bulky plane was used both for reconnaissance and as a two-seater hunter. As its engine lay exposed to an attack from the rear, it had to be escorted by lighter fighters, such as the recent Sopwith Pup. *(BA)*

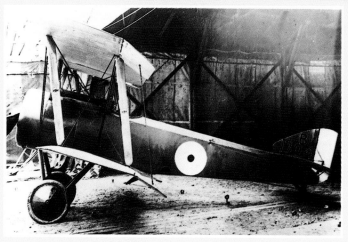

◄ A Sopwith Pup.

The small hunter was a blueprint for the famous Sopwith Camel that came later in the war. While less powerful, it was also much easier to fly. With the Sopwith Triplane used by the RNAS, it was the most efficient British hunter by far during the battle of Arras. But a very limited number was available, and on the western front it was used only by Squadrons 46, 54 and 66. *(MAP)*

The Albatros airplanes
of Jasta 5 at Boistrancourt in 1917.

Aircraft specialists will identify these as
D V models, which were not yet in service
at the time of the battle of Arras. But we have
no photographs of this unit with D IIIs. The
British were clearly superior in the air, as they
had 754 operational aircraft at the date of
April 9, 1917, while the Germans could only

line up 264 on that part of the front.
As far as single-seater hunters were
concerned, the ratio was 385 to 114 only.
However the Albatros D III was a much better
airplane, and even before the British had
launched their attack they had suffered heavy
losses. In the five days before 9 April, for
instance, the RFC lost 75 planes to the
enemy, with another 56 that crashed because
of bad weather or the pilots' lack of training.

The British airmen's life expectancy was
tragically short in April 1917, with a mere
23 days. True, some went into battle after
only 10 hours of solo flight. The superior
numbers did not compensate a technical
inferiority.
(Bundesarchiv)

◄ A German reconnaissance
plane forced to land
in Canadian lines.

It would be a mistake
to think that the heavy British
losses were only the result
of technical inadequacy.
Actually the British were much
more offensive than the Germans,
whose planes rarely ventured
above allied lines lest they
should meet this aircraft's fate.
Further evidence of this can be
found in the fact that general
Haig's attack came as a
complete surprise, in spite of
rather obvious preparations.
Also, it should be remembered
that the British were put at a
disadvantage by the dominant
westerly winds that pushed
their planes eastwards, far
behind the German lines,
particularly during dog fights.
(IWM)

A Minenwerfer is being
set up on a training ground. ▲

**This is a gun with removable
wheels, which made it possible to
give it a steady position in
trenches. One of the wheels can be
seen on the left. The Germans had
several hundreds of these guns
along the British front, north and
south of the scarpe.**
(IWM)

Unlimbering of ▶
several 77-mm guns.

**The units of
Kronprinz Rupprecht facing British
forces had the following guns:
- 419 77- and 90-mm guns;
- 240 105-mm howitzers;
- 118 guns with a calibre
ranging from 100 to 130 mm;
- 148 howitzers with a calibre
ranging from 150 to 199 mm;
- 74 200-mm howitzers;
for a total of 999 pieces.**

**On the other side,
the Third and First Armies
lined up 2, 817 guns, including:
- 1,404 18-pdr guns;
- 450 4.5-inch howitzers;
- 258 60-pdr guns;
- 364 6-inch howitzers;
- 40 6-inch guns;
- 124 8-inch howitzers;
- 148 9.2-inch howitzers;
- 2 9.2-inch guns;
- 17 12-inch howitzers;
- 2 12-inch guns;
- 8 15-inch howitzers.
The Germans were completely
outnumbered.**
(IWM)

◄ Entrance to a gallery at Riancourt, April 1917.

The Germans took advantage of underground opportunities too. The sign nailed to the tree bears the inscription: Katakomben, Eingang N° 2, or Catacombs, entrance n° 2.
(Bundesarchiv)

The forces of Kronprinz Rupprecht of Bavaria

Next pages.

This view of the battlefield gives a perfect idea of the Arras operation. The Hindenburg line has been ruptured and the British army is on open ground. Six 60-pdr guns are being set up, while a Female Tank is moving east. Cavalry can be seen in the background. Had the British at last come «To the green fields beyond» ?
(IWM)

9 April 1917 on the Third Army's front

EASTER Monday, 1917, will remain as one of the brightest days for the British army in the first world war. It was not only the most powerful offensive they had ever launched but also the most successful so far. While the number of attacking divisions - 14 - was the same as on 1 July 1916 on the Somme, the artillery support was unmatched, as shown before.

On the morning of 9 April, the advanced zone of the third Army was literally congested with troops: 200,000 infantry and artillery, engineers and tankers, backed by an impressive reserve of 150,000 men, including more infantry and cavalry ready to move into the battle when the front was broken through. Two-thirds of the battalions were on the first line, and the British feared until the very last minute that they might be spotted and shelled by the German artillery, which would have caused dire losses. But the German command did not expect the British attack until a week later, possibly because they knew the approximate date for the French offensive and thought both would be launched at the same time. Moreover German observers had had to remain under shelter for several days as a consequence of the mighty preliminary shelling. Their observation planes were clearly outnumbered and did not dare to venture above allied lines. Very few could slip through the net.

Weather was poor on 9 April, after a lull on Easter Sunday. There were occasional, sometimes strong, snow showers. The westerly wind blew snow into the German defenders' eyes, which of course was an

9 April 1917: a Mark II tank has fallen into a communication trench.

Contrary to what the high command hoped, the tanks found it extremely difficult to get out of the British lines. *(IWM)*

A superb view of a Male tank ▶ bogged down somewhere along the Fampoux road.

The picture was taken on terrain taken from the Germans on 9 April. Fampoux lies on the river Scarpe. *(IWM)*

advantage, although the snow, hail and rain had turned the roads into bogs. In many trenches the men were standing knee-deep in liquid mud, and some tanks were unable to move beyond the first British line. The soldiers were soaked through and frozen, all the more so as general Allenby had ordered them to leave their coats behind so as not to be slowed down by extra weight. But morale was high and determination unfailing.

The British assault was staggered over the day and began later on the front's right wing than on the centre or left. Some units went into the attack as early as 5:30 a.m., others after 4:00 p.m. only. We will work up north, starting with the rightmost units.

The right wing has to face a difficult situation

Support infantry going into battle, 9 April. ▶

On the right wing, the 21st Division attacked at 4:15 p.m. over a 3,000 yard wide front. The 64th Brigade was leading the way, with 1/East Yorkshire, 15/Durham LI and 9/KOYLI. They had to proceed in columns, as seen on the photo, because breaches in the wire of the Hindenburg line were few. The German barrage was quick but weak, a consequence of the British artillery's work. The first line was reached and crossed after 1,000 yards. But the second line's wire still stood intact. *(IWM)*

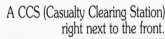

A CCS (Casualty Clearing Station)
right next to the front.

This advanced post, not far from
Tilloy-les-Mofflaines, gave the wounded first aid
before they were evacuated behind the lines.
Only the most serious cases were treated here.
All the men seen lying on stretchers are covered
with blankets, which could mean they are dead.
On the other hand the wounded may simply have
been sheltered from that day's bitter cold.
(IWM)

A support unit is entering the no-man's-land.

As 9/KOYLI could not find a breech in the enemy's first
line wire, all they could do was stand nearby, in spite of several
counter-attacks. The 21st Division was thus able to take only
two-thirds of the German first line. To the left, the 30th Division
was held in check too. A preliminary operation, at 1:30 a.m.,
permitted the capture of the village of Saint-Martin, but later in the
afternoon 19/King's and 20/King's were unable to enter
the Hindenburg line. German fire knocked down 200 men
in each battalion. The others crouched in the no-man's-land before
retreating to their starting position in the dark. The 21st Brigade's
attack to the north was just as unsuccessful. It was stopped
before the enemy wire by very heavy machine-gun fire: in 2/Wiltshire
only 342 men were downed. The four tanks assigned to
the 30th Division all got bogged down before reaching
the German line. The division's failure, however,
was untypical of what was going on elsewhere.
(IWM)

41

The first German prisoners being taken back to the British lines. ►

The 168th Brigade, on the left, met a similar success. The German barrage hit the starting position too late. After being held up for a while by the wire, the men of 12/London rushed forward after a tank had crushed it.

Two London battalions walked through Neuville-Vitasse, then on to the Hindenburg line from 12:10 p.m. 14/London (London Scottish) hesitated slightly on the direction, before successfully entering the Hindenburg line, capturing 3 lines in a row and 150 prisoners, and coming out onto open terrain. As they had gained over 600 yards, the men started worrying at their brilliant success and took shelter in the German trenches they had just conquered after a grenade mopping-up operation. The 56th Division advanced 1 1/4 mile, taking 612 German soldiers and losing 882 men. The support brigade was unharmed. *(IWM)*

Success for the 56th Division

A corporal of the Machine Gun Corps has just set up his gun in a conquered trench. ►

On the 167th Brigade's front, 3/London took the mill at Neuville, proceeded through the village itself, following close on the artillery's creeping barrage, and reached its final objective, the Blue Line. On its left, 8/Middlesex faced greater difficulty in the other part of Neuville-Vitasse, particularly because an enemy resistance pocket that lay hidden behind houses had not been destroyed by the artillery. After a hard fight the position was captured along with 68 prisoners and 4 machine-guns. But then contact was lost with the artillery barrage, and 8/Middlesex had a hard time, finally reaching the Blue Line at around 4:00 p.m. Meanwhile 1/London had already arrived in support. *(IWM)*

German gunners are dragging their heavy machine-gun into the British lines.

The 14th Division had been assigned a particularly difficult task: taking the Hindenburg line where it met with the former German defense system, which was guarded by a redoubt that the British called The Harp and by the slopes of Telegraph Hill. The division was supported by 14 tanks of battalions C and D.
(IWM)

A makeshift dug-out inside the German lines.

6/KOYLI and 10/Durham LI suffered heavy losses but captured the Hindenburg line.
(IWM)

The 14th Division in battle

After taking the Hindenburg line,
men of the 14th Division tried
to launch an attack against the
Wancourt-Feuchy line, but too
late as night was falling.
Losses in VII. Corps amounted
to about 1,000 per division.
(IWM)

◄ A party of forward artillery
observers directing British
fire during the battle
of the Scarpe.

Support shelling for the
14th Division was supplied
by the 13th and 37th Divisions'
ordnance, which was made up of
five groups. Their fire was so
accurate and powerful that the
British were surprised to see
German morale collapsing on
their section of the front. In many
instances the Germans remained
crouching in deep dug-outs,
without attempting to fire back,
and waited to surrender to
the first British waves.
(IWM)

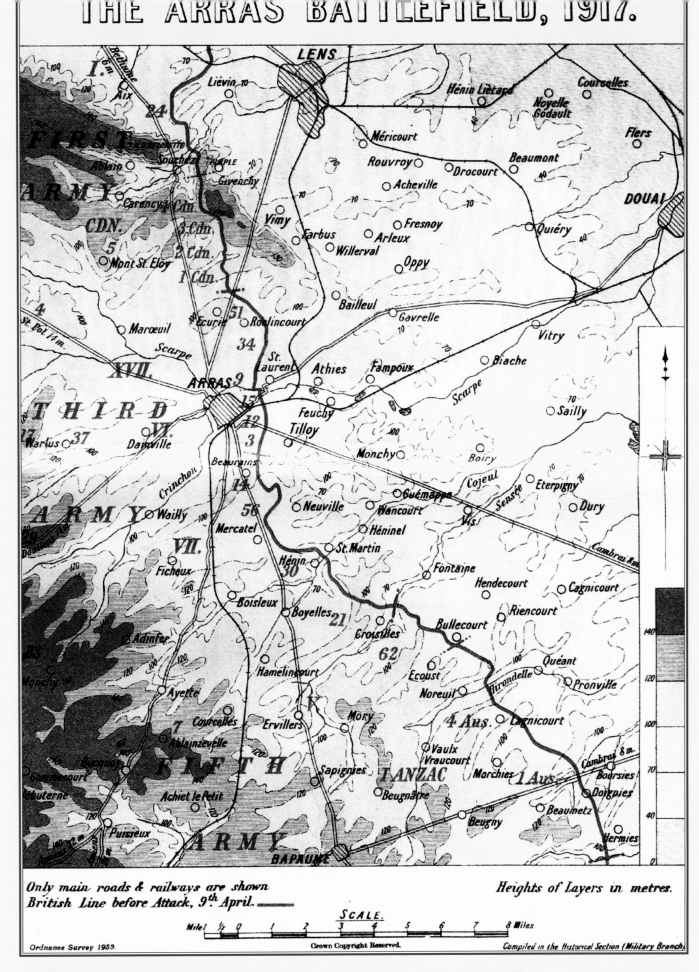

Only main roads & railways are shown
British Line before Attack, 9th April. ―――――

Heights of Layers in metres.

SCALE.

Mile ½ 0 1 2 3 4 5 6 7 8 Miles

Ordnance Survey 1939.

Crown Copyright Reserved.

Compiled in the Historical Section (Military Branch)

The British front in Arras on the morning of 9 April

is attacking

An artillery convoy in the ruins of Athies, on the banks of the Scarpe. ▶

Unlike VII. Corps, VI. Corps attacked from the former British lines and was consequently not handicapped by the German retreat. Its communication lines were not as clogged, one reason being that it could use a narrow-gauge line capable of ferrying 100 tons of heavy ammo daily. This allowed to divert heavy traffic from the roads. The caissons seen here were only transporting medium-calibre shells. VI. Corps' target was first to capture the Hindenburg line, or rather the main German line which in this place lay in front of it, then to move on to the Wancourt-Feuchy, or Brown, line. *(IWM)*

An artillery ammo convoy on the Arras-Cambrai road, close to Tilloy-les-Mofflaines.

The 8th Brigade joined the battle in the afternoon of 9 April and forced the last defenders of Tilloy to capitulate, with 136 men surrendering. British troops continued their advance up to about 600 yards away from the Wancourt-Feuchy line, where machine-gun fire from the Chapel at Feuchy obliged them to stop. *(IWM)* ▼

Near the Feuchy road junction,
a KRRC convoy is delivering officers' clothing. ▲

▼ Heliograph signalling
in Feuchy, south of the Scarpe.

An airplane was probably flying overhead, as several officers
can be seen looking up. At about 6:45 p.m., after serious artillery
preparation, 1/Gordon Highlanders attempted to reach the Wancourt-
Feuchy line, but was once again kept away from German defenses by
machine-guns at the Feuchy chapel. 8/King's Own, coming from far
behind, was too late to help the Scots. Still, the enemy's main line
was captured on the whole of the 3rd Division's front.
On the left, the 12th Division attacked in very favourable conditions,
with the men coming out of underground galleries and caves which led
from the cathedral's crypt to the German first line in complete safety.
(IWM)

VI. Corps was made up, from right to left, of
the 3rd, 12th and 15th Divisions. The 3rd had
the support of 117 howitzers and 43 guns.
In this sector the attack was launched at
5:30 a.m. Success was complete, as all targets
were met on time, except around Tilloy where
the Germans held on to the château and a
neighbouring quarry. One tank only came to
help 13/King's. The other nine of
the 9th Company were bogged down.
(IWM)

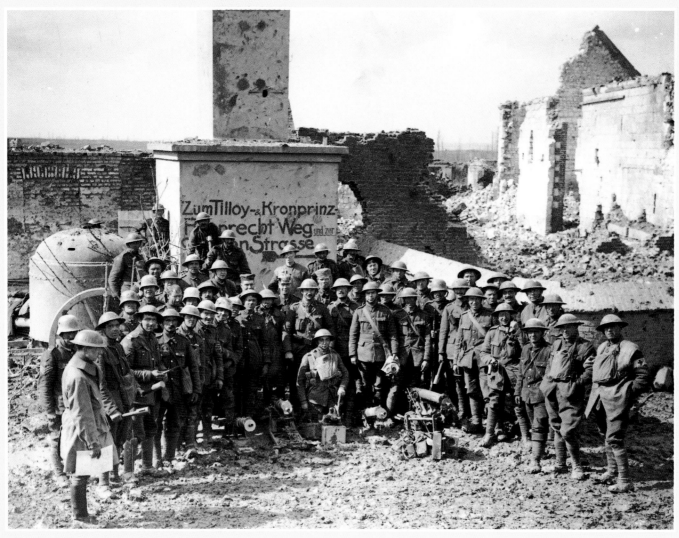

The 13 King's Liverpool Regiment in Tilloy. ▲

The men are posing in front of a German concrete observation tower and a mobile armoured observation unit.
They are displaying a number of trophies: stick grenades, machine-guns, spiked helmets and steel helmets, etc.
(IWM)

Major achievements of the 12th Division

Men of the Machine Gun Corps in battle.

They are seen here shooting at a plane. 37th Brigade's advance was supported by a barrage of 24 Vickers like this one, firing over the 6/Queen's and 7/East Surrey's assault waves.
(IWM) ▶

Two guns taken from the Germans in the vicinity of Feuchy.

The village lay in ruins, but the trees lining the Scarpe were still standing: breaking through the German front, 12th Division infantry won Observation Ridge after a hard-fought battle and was able to go down into Battery Valley. Here, 9/Essex and 5/Royal Bershire achieved an incredible feat: for the first time since the beginning of trench warfare, two battalions came out onto open terrain and charged at enemy artillery. Many German gunners ran away, but a few kept their heads and fired point-blank at the infantry until they were overwhelmed in true Napoleonic fashion.
(IWM)

A 77-mm gun is being unlimbered against its former owners.

Altogether, Essex took nine German guns and Royal Bershire no less than twenty-two, some of which were used immediately.
(IWM)

49

Reserves in the the battle

Supply columns are going up to the front, first past pionneers building a new road, then past a CCS.

In spite of their success at Battery Valley, the infantry could not keep up with the creeping fire and were too late when they came to face the Wancourt-Feuchy line. They were pushed back. The 37th Division, until then in reserve, was sent into the fight. Going through Arras on three different roads, it arrived on the battlefield at noon. At about 6:00 p.m., one brigade met the fire of machine-guns on the Wancourt-Feuchy line. Night was falling and the troops, although fresh, could not get through. ▶
(IWM) ▼

Digging a communication
trench between Tilloy and Feuchy. ▲

**Their resistance on the Wancourt-
Feuchy line spared the Germans
a complete breakdown of the front.**
(IWM)

German stretcher-bearers
are putting down a wounded man.

**Although many Germans were
taken prisoners south of the Scarpe,
the vital Wancourt-Feuchy line
was fiercely defended.**
▼
(IWM)

A captured 77-mm gun
firing at the German lines ▲

**While some of the guns taken
in Battery Valley were being turned
against the Brown Line's defenders,
the 15th Division south of the
Scarpe achieved the day's most
brilliant feat. The four front
battalions, all of them from Scotland,
took the enemy position without
fighting, then the 40th Brigade
rushed into Battery Alley and,
despite heavy losses, overwhelmed
and captured 36 German guns.
Success was such that the cavalry
was called in. Meanwhile Feuchy was
being heavily shelled in preparation.
(IWM)**

Taking a break
in the ruins of Feuchy. ►

**Shortly after 4 p.m., the
15th Division managed to get a
foothold on the Wancourt-Feuchy line
and half an hour later had
captured the whole of it on its
attacking front, with the help of a
single tank that had miraculously got
there. A few prisoners were taken on
the Brown Line, pushing the day's
total up to 500 for the 15th Division.
To take advantage of the situation,
the 63rd Brigade was launched into
the battle. Unfortunately it came
from far back, but still managed to
capture Orange Hill at nightfall and
without fighting, some three miles
away from the British lines! (IWM)**

The last German line is broken!

A mule convoy about to leave Arras to the first lines.

This was obviously not cavalry, which in any case played a small part on the first day.
(IWM)

Modern cavalry is bogged in trenches and horse cavalry is on standby.

Although it could not exploit the breakthrough in the 15th's Division sector, VI. Corps cavalry did take part in the battle on 9 April when the Northamptonshire Yeomanry moved beyond the village of Feuchy recently captured by infantry and on to the junction south of the Scarpe, in Fampoux, taking six guns, knocking down snipers and joining with units of XVII. Corps that were successfully operating north of the river.
(IWM)

▲

Two views of
Happy Valley ►

The success of XVII. Corps
north of the Scarpe was
outstanding. The final
objective of Z day was the
so-called Point-du-Jour line.
It was reached by the
9th Division, attacking north
of the Scarpe, over all its
front. Official British records
read: " *Athies, heavily
bombarded but still standing,
collapsed and dissolved into
powder before the eyes of the
advancing infantry*". By
8 p.m., the division had taken
51 officers and 2,047 men.
The 4th Division was
immediately thrown into the
fight and, although coming
from far back, was able to
take the village of Fampoux,
where it was joined by VI.
Corps cavalry.
Its 12th Brigade, which had
captured 230 prisoners and
24 guns, including 10 15-cm
howitzers (two of which are
seen here), lost only 147 men.
The 11th Brigade was even
more successful: not only did
it secure the Oppy-Méricourt
line, but it gained almost four
miles - the greatest advance
in a single day since the
trench war had started.
(IWM)

A 150-mm howitzer captured on 9 April 1917.

The attack was equally successful on the front of the 34th Division. The Germans even fled from the Point du Jour line, leaving everything behind. But the division's left wing was stopped by the enemy and the situation remained confused until nightfall. In fact, almost all the objectives had been reached.
(IWM)

German prisoners carrying a wounded man in Arras.

The 51st (Highland) Division was placed at the northern end of the Third Army's front of attack. It faced greater difficulties than the other divisions of XVII. Corps and the Scots did not reach their final objective, because of early losses and also because of orientation problems. All the same, the division captured 700 prisoners, 2 field guns and 29 machine-guns.
(IWM)

The offensive north of the Scarpe

A promising start

◄ A British stretcher-bearer giving water to a wounded German soldier.

At the end of the day, the Third Army informed marshal Haig that it had counted 5,600 prisoners and 36 guns taken from the enemy. Actually, once the final tally was completed, the British realized they had conquered over 100 guns and taken more than 11,000 German prisoners. Considerable ground had been gained, as was seen before, but the greatest success had not come where the high command expected it, so that the cavalry could not be used. It is likely that, if it had been able to take advantage of the breakthrough of XVII. Corps, it would have obtained surprisingly good results. All the infantry officers who called for the cavalry agreed: " Tomorrow will be too late! "
(IWM)

An Advanced Dressing Station near Tilloy.

British losses were light if measured against achievements and the experience of previous offensives. They were estimated to half those of the Germans.

The latter suffered hugely, as each of the first line battalions was destroyed and the support battalion also had losses. Resistance became stiffer when the third battalion arrived from behind the lines.
(IWM)

▼

Some of the 11,000 German prisoners of 9 April 1917. ►

The British offensive had dealt a very severe blow to German forces. However, nothing was settled on the evening of 9 April and the Germans could still recover. *(IWM)*

The Canadian offensive at Vimy

Wounded men are evacuated on a narrow gauge track. ▲

Work on their hinterland allowed the Canadians quick evacuation of the wounded.(IWM)

UNLIKE the Arras area, the Vimy and Notre-Dame de Lorette sectors were not new battlefields. On the contrary, this had been the most disputed ground in France since the fights of late 1914, when 150,000 men were lost (killed, wounded or missing) on the French side. The terrible attacks, led by general Pétain with insufficient artillery support, had nevertheless permitted to loosen the Germans' hold on that sector - a hold that was all the stronger as the Vimy position was a key element in the defense of the coal mining area around Lens and the plain of Douai.

While the 1915 offensives had not given the French control of the Labyrinth stronghold near Ecurie, south of the ridge, more substantial progress had been acomplished north of this when Carency and Neuville-Saint-Vaast were taken, along with Ablain-Saint-Nazaire and Souchez in the Souchez valley. Further north, the plateau of Notre-Dame de Lorette had been conquered after a dreadful fight, with the exception of Bois en Hache at its easternmost end.

From 1916 onwards, the front was quiet again and the Germans kept building up their defenses, although their situation was far less favourable than in october 1914: they held on to Bois en Hache but their defenses lacked depth, with considerably reduced space on the Vimy ridge proper. In the event of a fresh offensive, the assailants' task would be easier, thanks to the gruesome sacrifices of 1915. Also, the French had learnt useful lessons from past failures, particularly concerning the absolute need for heavy artillery on a terrain that had many deep underground galleries - some of which reputed-

ly dating back to the religious wars - used for shelter by the Germans.

Early in 1917 it became evident that the Third Army's offensive at Arras would be at risk should the Vimy ridge on its left flank remain under German control. Accordingly general Home's First Army prepared an assault against both Vimy, to the south, and Bois en Hache and Hill 13 - known in British ranks as The Pimple - to the north.

As the Vimy ridge was the more difficult objective, the Canadian corps' four divisions, helped by the 5th (British) Division's 13th Brigade, were deployed there. The northern attack was to be carried out by the 24th British Division, supported by the leftmost Canadian division.

The Canadian corps placed their four divisions in numerical order (1 to 4) from right to left facing Vimy. Of course their attack had to be synchronized with the Third Army's. As the front had a very irregular shape, the task would be widely different depending on where the attack was launched: on the right, the objective was 2.5 miles away, while on the left, where the front was shorter, [cote 145] was less than 800 yards from the first Canadian line. The attack was to be staggered and the ridge secured by Zero + 7:48 hours.

Canadian gunners are unlimbering their Vickers in shell holes.

The picture was taken on the Vimy ridge - today a very different sight after complete reforestation. Machine guns were one of the favourite weapons on both sides in 1917. Far was the time when general Haig wrote that in his opinion 2 machine-guns were enough per battalion. The creation of the Machine Gun Corps in 1915 showed that he was able to adapt.
(IWM)

General Julian Byng.

After commanding the Canadians in 1917, he was to lead the famous offensive at Cambrai in November.
(IWM)

A 12-inch howitzer
of the Canadian Corps.

**The Canadian Corps had
245 heavy guns, which were
to be complemented by the
First Army's 58 and the
1st Corps' 28 heavy batteries
siège The Canadians had
4 12-inch howitzers and
were given four more for the
operation, as well as one gun
of a similar calibre.**
(IWM)

Canadian
preparations

A heavy [naval gun] opens
fire against German positions.

**Altogether, there was one gun
or howitzer every 65 feet on
the Canadian front.**
(IWM)

Artillery ammo supplies
for the 20th Canadian Field Battery. ▲

For the coming battle, a total of 42,609 tonnes
of ammunition and 2,465 tonnes of daily rations
had been put together for the Canadian Corps
and the 1st Corps. The Canadian Corps' field
artillery was made up of 30 brigades, with
480 18-pdr guns and 138 4.5-inch howitzers.
(IWM)

A naval gun
about to open fire.

The presence of naval guns here is
explained by the fact that the
63rd (Royal Naval) Division had lent
their artillery to the Canadian corps.
The offensives plan of their
artillery was similar to the
Third Army's.*(IWM)*
▼

A German ammunition dump explodes after being hit by Canadian artillery.

On the First Army's front, the artillery preparation began on 20 March, almost two weeks before the Third Army's. Stage two, which the Germans dubbed "the week of suffering", opened on 2nd April with all available guns. Its aim was to destroy the wire (as seen below) and fire was concentrated against Thélus, Les Tilleuls, Farbus and other villages in the sector.
(IWM)

Preliminary shelling

A wrected German ▶
15-cm gun in its concrete shelter.

The Canadian and British counter-battery fire was formidable: the 4.5-inch howitzers shot 18,500 shells at the enemy artillery, the 60-pdr guns no less than 87,000, and the 9.2-inch howitzers 12,600. To this must be added some 7,800 6-inch shells.
(IWM)

The heaps of cases and empty boxes are a clear indication of how intense the artillery preparation was.

The 18-pdr guns, for example, fired 155,000 shells between March 20 and April 2, and again 492,000 from April 2 to 9. The 6-inch howitzers fired 39,600 shots, then 102,000, in the same periods. Moreover the 280 machine-guns of the Canadian Machine Gun Corps kept firing at night. Almost one million shells were delevered at the Vimy ridge - a total of 50,000 tonnes of steel and other metals. The fine trench network was utterly ruined.
(IWM) ▼

This Canadian ambulance was hit twice in six months.

In spite of their losses, the Canadians still outnumbered the Germans. The German units had suffered much more, and only 5,000 men were facing the 15,000 Canadians of the first assault waves. *(IWM)*

The German riposte

Canadian soldiers shelter in a trench during a German shelling.

Of course the Germans did not remain passive during the long artillery preparation. It seems that a Bavarian regiment was planning to launch a preventive attack after a gas shelling, but this had to be cancelled when winds started to blow from the west. In any case the German artillery response was lethal: in the two weeks from March 22 to April 5, the Canadians had 11 officers and 326 men killed, with 60 officers and 1,256 men wounded or missing. *(IWM)* ▼

A carrier pigeon is released from a first line trench.

On the right, the lieutenant who has just written the message - he is still holding a pen - watches the bird's flight. On the eve of battle, the Canadians were crowding the trenches: in addition to the 15,000 men of the first assault waves there were as many in support units - a total of 52 battalions or 30,000 men on a four-mile front.
(IWM)

Canadian soldiers trying to extricate an ammo truck from the mud.

The heavy shells lying on a narrow-gauge track seem to have unloaded from the truck. All batteries had to be supplied as quickly as possible for the huge ammo consumption that was planned on the 9th, in order both to destroy the enemy's first line and to silence the German batteries.
(IWM)

A British female tank
on the 2nd Canadian Division's
front, on the Vimy ridge. ▶

There were few tanks on the
Third Army's front at Arras,
and even fewer in the Canadian
Corps: only eight were assigned
to support the 2nd Division.
They were to help in the assault
against the fortified village of
Thélus. But no one trusted their
ability to handle the upturned and
muddy terrain, so that neither
the infantry nor the artillery plan
made any provisions for the eight
tanks. Photographers alone,
after all, seemed to take an
interest in them...
(IWM)

Attacking the Vimy ridge

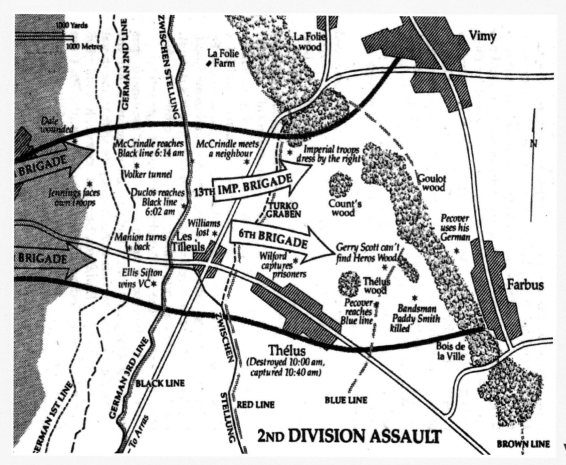

2ND DIVISION ASSAULT

Labels on map:
1000 Yards
1000 Metres
GERMAN 2ND LINE
ZWISCHEN STELLUNG
La Folie wood
La Folie Farm
Vimy
Dale wounded
BRIGADE
McCrindle reaches Black line 6:14 am
McCrindle meets a neighbour
Imperial troops dress by the right
Goulot wood
Volker tunnel
Jennings faces own troops
13TH IMP. BRIGADE
Duclos reaches Black line 6:02 am
TURKO GRABEN
Count's wood
Pecover uses his German
Williams lost
6TH BRIGADE
Manion turns back
Les Tilleuls
Gerry Scott can't find Heros Wood
BRIGADE
Ellis Sifton wins VC
Wilford captures prisoners
Thélus wood
Farbus
Pecover reaches Blue line
Bandsman Paddy Smith killed
Bois de la Ville
GERMAN 3RD LINE
ZWISCHEN STELLUNG
Thélus (Destroyed 10:00 am, captured 10:40 am)
BLACK LINE
To Arras
RED LINE
BLUE LINE
BROWN LINE
GERMAN 1ST LINE
N

Canadian progress on the Vimy ridge.

While Canadian soldiers are moving forward on badly shelled terrain, German soldiers are leaving their shelters, "only to happy to surrender" as the original caption would have it. On the 1st Division's right wing, the Canadians reached the first German line even before the defenders had abandoned their shelters. On the left wing, three German machine guns caused some losses before they were destroyed. The two brigades moved on, following on the barrage. With occasionally heavy losses due to the courage of some isolated German gunners, the 1st Division reached its objective after only half an hour. Shortly after 7 a.m. the second objective, the intermediary line, was secured. Success was complete so far and the 2nd Division, on the left, won a similar victory.
(IWM)

The 2nd Canadian Division's assault

Two views showing a few of the 2nd Division's eight tanks about to move into the battle. ▲

On this division's front, German resistance showed more resolve. The 18th (Western Ontario) Battalion suffered severe losses from two machine guns. One of them was overpowered by Sergeant Sifton who rushed forward on his own with fixed bayonet and stabbed at the enemy gunners. The incredible feat was not to bring him luck however, as he was killed some time later and awarded the Victoria Cross posthumously.
In front of the second German line, it took much daring and courage again from the Canadians to win the day. After a forty minute break, the division moved on, took Les Tilleuls or what was left of it, and reached the intermediary line behind the village. Among the ruins, the Canadians found a large cave where they captured six officers and about a hundred men belonging to the staff of two battalions. The village of Thélus and hill 135 were then looming just in front of the first assault waves.
(IWM) ▼

◀ A piece of ordnance taken from the Germans in a bunker.

The concrete of German bunkers in the Great War did not have the sleek appearance of the Todt organisation's constructions. This might look more like a cave, but the pieces of steel framework leave no doubt. The badly shattered gun is an old model, as far as can be seen. *(IWM)*

Double page suivante
On the Vimy ridge: German soldiers surrendering and going back to the rear.

Live battle shots are uncommon in all conflicts, be it the Great War or the Gulf war. Pictures like this one are therefore of great value. (IWM)

The 2nd Division moving towards its objective.

Ahead of the 5th Brigade, the 25th (Nova Scotia Rifles) Battalion reached its target early on: this was the Turko-Graben, a name reminiscent of the times when French colonial troops had fought in the sector. The Canadians captured 390 prisoners and 4 machine guns.
(IWM)

▼

◀ An artillery position taken from the enemy on the front at Vimy.

A 15-cm howitzer has been taken out of its shelter in La Folie wood. ▲

A similar howitzer firing at the Germans.

The 3rd Division, pouring out of long tunnels (Goodman, 2,000 yards, and Grange, 1,400 yards), arrived in front of the German lines without being spotted. The gunners were captured even before they could open fire. The Canadian's advance was so fast that they ran into their own artillery barrage. After a pause they moved on, took the farm at La Folie and fought vigorously in the wood of the same name. Losses were severe, all the more as men of Reserve Infanterie Regiment 262 counter-attacked twice with grenades. The wood was eventually secured, even though there remained German snipers. Thus the Vimy ridge was completely subdued in this sector. *(IWM)*

It has been turned back at the German lines and is ready to open fire, as the Canadians have found some ammo among the empty boxes. *(IWM)*

The Canadians gained ground so fast that they were able to collect a lot of equipment from the enemy. *(IWM)*

▼

The Third Division in battle

Canadians burying down in the third German line.

The Vimy ridge might as well be called a plateau, being flat on ◀ the side of the Canadian assault. *(IWM)*

A large number of
German prisoners are walking
down from the Vimy ridge.

**Quick progress on part of the
4th Division's front gave the
Canadians many prisoners.
On the right, the 54th (Central
Ontario) Battalion passed hill
145, but the Canadian Grenadier
Guards were held back by
machine gun fire from the top.**
(IWM)

The 4th
Division
in front
of hill 145

Canadian soldiers attempting
to contact the air force.

**On the left of the front, the
Vimy ridge had been captured
by 7 a.m.**
(IWM)

Two men of
the Royal Engineers are
examining a skull found
on the battlefield.

The Germans had made the
same mistake as in Verdun four
months before by their first line
crammed with troops who were
either killed or captured in their
shelters. On 9 April the number
of prisoners made by the
Canadians was 62 officers
and 3,342 men.
(IWM)

A German naval gun
captured near Vimy.

By 7 a.m., the whole of
the German defense front had
been captured, with the
exception of a strip of ground
near hill 145. Almost everywhere,
the assault waves could have
moved on, but the artillery
barrage had been set for a slow
and methodical advance
which left no room for
surprise attacks.
(IWM)

A tank is being cheered as it returns from battle.

If the original caption is authentic, this picture must have been arranged by the photographer, as tanks took no part in the battle of Vimy. The eight tanks of the 12th Company, D Battalion, were to attack as follows: a frontal attack by four and two encircling movements on each wing for two more. The last two were supposed to attack Count's wood, on the 13th Brigade front, but none of them managed to get across the no-man's-land which, admittedly, had turned into a bog..
(IWM)

The capture of Thélus

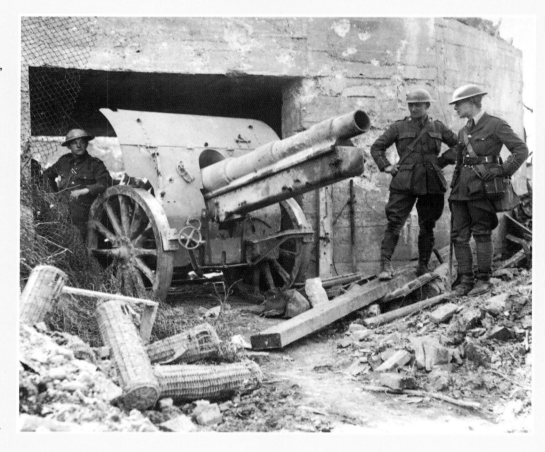

A 15-cm German howitzer taken from the Germans in its bunker.

After the 31st (Alberta) and 28th (North West) Battalions had secured Thélus, the Canadians came up against a line of concrete bunkers, at the higher ends of [bois de la Ville] and Farbus wood. They moved up behind the artillery barrage and were able to subdue the German defense line and take many guns.
(IWM)

Part of the Canadian's
bounty from the Vimy ridge.

The Canadians took a large number
of machine guns. This photo shows
only some of them, but almost a
hundred are on display. In the
evening of 9 April, the whole of the
Vimy ridge had been conquered
except hill 145. The 27th (City of
Winnipeg) Battalion captured an
artillery battery, where it made
250 prisoners including the
commander and staff of Bayerische
Reserve Regiment 3. Patrols were
even sent down the ridge into
the plain of Douai, towards the
small station wood and around
the village of Farbus. (IWM)

Two wounded Canadians
on their way to Blighty.

From the bandages it can be
supposed they were severely burnt.
Losses were far from negligible on
the Canadian side, amounting
to 11,297 men between 7 and
14 April 1917. The most severely
harmed brigade was the 12th, with
317 men killed, 891 wounded
and 136 missing. Then came the
2nd Brigade, with 279 killed,
800 wounded and 39 missing.
(IWM)

Canadian infantry
in dug-outs on the Vimy ridge. ▶

Hill 145, a key position, was
the closest objective to Canadian
lines, hardly 800 yards away.
However it had not been captured
in the morning of 9 April, for
the German defenses were
particularly good there.
All morning, the 11th Brigade
suffered continuous losses under
enemy fire. Eventually an infantry
assault, with no artillery support,
got the best of it early in
the afternoon.
(IWM)

A view of Vimy from the ridge.

On the 10th, the Canadians
launched an assault against the
Hangstellung, a position halfway
down the slope. The Calgary
Battalion was able to subdue it
but lost 11 officers and 218 men.
Only the Pimple was still
German on the ridge. ▼
(IWM)

Assault on hill 145

◄ A triumphant return for Canadian soldiers.

The capture of hill 145 ended the battle of Vimy proper, as the Pimple was not really on it, but rather on an outlying hillock. In the same sector was bois en Hache, the last German bastion on the hill of Notre-Dame de Lorette. Both were attacked on the 12th in a snow storm. The Pimple fell into the 10th Canadian Brigade's hands at 5:45 a.m. Bois en Hache was captured with greater difficulty by British troops.
(IWM)

▼ The ruins of Farbus, below the Vimy ridge.

The conquest of the Vimy ridge was a superb success, but the Canadians still had to capitalize on it by going down into the plain of Douai.
(IWM)

The impossible breakthrough

I N order to capitalize on the victory of April 9, it was essential that the Brown Line be captured as soon as possible. General Allenby gave the order to take it on April 10 at 8:00 a.m., then to proceed to the Green Line. The cavalry was to be ready from 7:00 a.m. Progress was nevertheless much slower than the day before. The fine artillery setup was no more, and the Hindenburg line had not been mopped up everywhere. In some trenches, grenade fights had raged throughout the night. In the morning it was not easy to approach the Wancourt-Feuchy line. The Germans hadn't given up yet. On the 21st Division's front for example, a powerful German counter-attack, prepared by a violent minenwerfer bombardment, drove the 1/East Yorkshires from their trenches. The British decided against attempting a fresh assault, for which they were not ready.

On the 3rd and 12th Divisions' fronts, the movements of 10 April were successful: Orange Hill was completely captured by the 3rd Division. The 12th moved on towards Chapel Hill, near Feuchy, and secured it with relative ease, with the Germans fleeing at the last minute.

The 37th Division proceeded towards Monchy-le-Preux, a village sitting on top of a hill with a commanding view of the battlefield. The 8/Somerset Light Infantry reached Lone Copse Valley, but from then on could only hop from one shell hole to the next while the Germans fired at them from their higher position. This battalion's movements, with the 8/Lincolshire's and 4/Middlesex's, could be followed from Orange Hill and their progression seemed good enough to advise the cavalry of the opportunity for a breakthrough. Actually the attack was much slower than it looked. The infantry, for one thing, was hindered by the fact that the field artillery and Royal

The success of 9 April was unprecedented, but in order to take advantage of it it was necessary to move fast in the hours following the breaking of the front. Would the men's enthusiasm be enough? Could the artillery be redeployed in time?
(IWM)

Horse Artillery were on the move and could not help. Only heavy batteries were pounding at Monchy. The Germans, on the other hand, suffered no such handicap and their artillery's enfilade fire from north of the Scarpe was particularly damaging. About 500 yards from Monchy, British infantry found any advance impossible.

However the Wancourt-Feuchy line, which the day before remained almost intact, was everywhere captured by 10 April. Some British units, such as the 8/East Lincolnshire, went one mile further on.

This allowed the cavalry to approach the first lines. Shortly before noon, it was ordered to move east of Arras and to proceed on the road to Cambrai. Congested roads did not make its task easy. General Greenly, the commanding officer of the 2nd Cavalry Division, ordered his 3rd and 5th Cavalry Brigades to move to a position west of the Wancourt-Feuchy line, just south of Orange Hill. The 3rd Brigade was immediately stopped by machine guns from hill 90. As a consequence, the division could not join the fight and was ordered to be prepared for the following day.

German prisoners
on the streets of Arras. ▲

**Hatred of the Hun or Boche
is a figment of the journalists'
imagination. Of course the men
entertained no warm feelings
toward their enemies, but they
did not despise them, knowing
their skill in fighting.
Also, sharing the same ordeal
could obviously make both
sides mutually sympathetic.
Fraternizing was seen early in the
war and much less often in 1917.
But reciprocal help, particularly
to rescue the wounded, was not
a rare sight.** *(IWM)*

A common grave at Vimy.

**Losses on 9 April were far from
negligible, with the consequence
that some units were weakened
or disorganized on the next day,
while the reserves were not
yet on the field.** *(IWM)* ▶

Two Rolls Royce ▶ armoured cars on a street in Arras.

Everything had been planned to exploit the victory of 9 April at the earliest opportunity, as is shown by these vehicles equipped with chains for muddy terrain. *(IWM)*

No possible break-through

British cavalry riding along the edge of a mine crater.

The 3rd Division was ordered to get to Vis-en-Artois and Boiry-Notre-Dame. But fire from Monchy blocked passage through the village. After a charge against Monchy failed, the cavalry had to thank the snow storm for being able to retreat with minor losses. *(IWM)* ▼

Men of the Manchester
Regiment getting ready
to work on conquered ground.

April 10 was a disappointing
day for Britain. True, the
Wancourt-Feuchy line was
completely captured and in
some cases units advanced by
more than one mile. But two
severe handicaps were
threatening the conclusion of
the battle: it had not been
possible to strike deep into the
enemy's lines, while large German
reinforcements were very likely
to arrive. Moreover British losses
were getting heavier, so that the
attack divisions were beginning
to lose their breath.
(IWM)

The ruins of a
German outpost.

The German reserve divisions,
left too far behind, could not be
sent into the fight on the first
day, leaving an impression of
impending disaster. On the other
hand fresh troops began to arrive
in the evening of April 10, and
the battle was now about to look
totally different.
(IWM)

A camouflaged
armoured car on the road
to Tilloy-les-Mofflaines.

The British faced a dilemma:
they could either replace the
exhausted divisions and lose
precious time, or keep them in
battle and run the risk of
insufficient power for victory.
(IWM)

In Arras, an ammunition dump explodes after being hit by German artillery.

The Germans clearly resumed a tougher line on April 10, even though the British advance continued north of the Scarpe as well. The Point-du-Jour line was conquered and Haig thought that if Monchy-le-Preux proved too formidable an obstacle for a frontal attack, the divisions placed north of the Scarpe could by-pass it and attack from the rear. But insufficient progress did not permit the manoeuvre. *(IWM)*

April 10 on the north bank of the Scarpe

British soldiers sheltering in a house taken on April 9.

The infantry now lacked the punch for a breakthrough. Accordingly the cavalry was ordered to rush at Gavrelle, Oppy and Vitry-en-Artois. But it came from far behind and did not approach the German lines until 4:30 p.m.., by which time snow showers prevented an attack. *(IWM)*

British infantry waiting to get into the battle.

Two of the men are seen wearing caps rather than their steel helmets, which probably means the enemy was not too close. Operations north of the Scarpe proved disappointing, as no real step was taken to take advantage of the previous day's breaking of the front, probably because initial orders were that the break-through would be attempted south of the river. Following orders too closely was of course detrimental to daring movements.
(IWM)

Field kitchens in formerly German lines.

The British accounted for their slow reaction on April 10 by blaming congested roads and their very poor condition due to bad weather, which prevented the artillery from moving forward.
(IWM)

Prince Arthur of Connaught, ▶
general Byng and a French liaison
officer are examining a large-
caliber shell in its wicker basket.

**On April 9 and 10,
the British army took 103 guns,
163 machine guns and 60 trench
mortars along with minenwerfers
of all sizes, some of which can be
seen at the back.**
(IWM)

The first
two days'
bounty

German prisoners
are bringing food rations
to the camp at Wanquetin.

**The British captured
11,000 prisoners in two days.** ▼
(IWM)

A very large caliber
Minenwerfer captured at Vimy.

The capture of the Vimy ridge
forced the Germans to give up
their downhill positions and they
began a significant retreat,
abandoning the mining town of
Liévin among others. They took
new positions south of Lens, in
front of Avion, thus forsaking any
hope of recapturing the Vimy
ridge. However the Canadians
could not exploit their advantage
as the terrain and road conditions
were even worse than on the
Scarpe, making any artillery
movement impossible.
And attacking the Oppy-Méricourt
line without artillery support
was out of the question, as
the Germans had received
reinforcements.
(IWM)

A prisoner of IR 76
in a trench facing Gravelle.

This regiment belonging to
the 17. Infanterie Division came
to relieve the remnants of
the 1. Bayer. Division in the
morning of April 10, together
with the 89. Grenadier Regiment.
By the 12th they were
operational, with their own
artillery and heavy guns.
(IWM)

Back from Monchy,
British troops are boarding
double-deckers to leave the front.

On 11 April, the British launched
their last breaching offensive
against the Drocourt-Quéant line.
General Allenby, in his Order of
the day, declared that the Third
Army was pursuing a defeated
enemy and that risks should be
taken, particularly in by-passing
the enemy's resistance pockets.
(IWM)

The capture of Monchy-le-Preux

▲ A field ambulance in action.

Losses were severe on April 11: while the enemy had been defeated in the previous days, they were not routed and the day's operations had nothing to do, by far, with a pursuit, as the Germans had managed to recover. British attacks were almost everywhere checked by units which, unlike them, were fresh. The 21st Division's failure was complete, like the 3rd Division's at Guémappe. The 2nd Cavalry Division was ready to attack but of course could not in the circumstances, and had to withdraw beyond Arras under shelling.
(IWM)

9.2-inch howitzers at Neuville-Vitasse.

The artillery had begun to redeploy, but in order to win the British had to renew their effort of April 9. They no longer had the means for this. Only the 37th Division was able to capture Monchy after a difficult battle, supported by four tanks of C Battalion which destroyed enemy machine gun positions and enabled an exhausted and decimated 13/Rifle Brigade to take and hold the village. The cavalry was immediately sent in, but the first squadrons were slaughtered by German artillery
(IWM)

The Australians in Bullecourt and the end of the British offensive

WHILE the Third Army was attacking around Arras and the First at Vimy, general Gough's Fifth was getting ready to launch a secondary offensive at Bullecourt, about 4 miles south of Vis-en-Artois. If victorious, this limited operation against the Hindenburg line would cause the German front to collapse west of the Drocourt-Quéant line, which would facilitate Allenby's victory on the Scarpe.

Gough would have liked to launch his offensive on the same day as the Third, but this was not possible for a number of reasons, one being that the Fifth Army was located on terrain that the Germans had laid to waste during the Alberich operation. It had just made contact with the enemy and its artillery was not ready. This obviously meant a delay: the heavy artillery had started to shell the wire between Bullecourt and Quéant, but this was 30 yards deep and no significant breach had been opened yet. Thus general Gough was sorry to hear from 1 Anzac, on 8 April, that eight more days of shelling would be needed to get rid of the wire. The operation had to be posponed by several days.

The Third Army launched its offensive on the 9th, and reports to general Gough showed it was highly successful. He too wished to have a share in the laurels of victory, but how? A suggestion was then put forward by lieutenant-colonel Hardress Lloyd, the commanding officer of D Tank Battalion: by using all of their eight tanks on a narrow front (only two-thirds of a mile), he was sure he could crush through the enemy wire and open the way to the Australian infantry. Rather unexpectedly, Gough showed interest, enthusiasm even, as he decided to try this as early as the next day. Orders were immediately dispatched

to all units concerned. The assault would be launched on April 11 at 4:30 a.m., i.e. almost two hours before daybreak: the initial attack had to be carried out in darkness as the terrain might be swept by machine guns located in Bullecourt and Quéant. The sector of attack was not a salient but a pocket, with obvious disadvantages.

At 1 a.m. on the 10th, Bullecourt was heavily gas-shelled and the two Australian brigades took positions in the trenches, awaiting the tanks. But the tanks were not materializing. Caught in a snow storm, they were seriously behind schedule. Daybreak was getting close and under the circumstances the assailants would be quickly spotted if no decision was taken. The operation was then delayed until the next day.

The tanks' attack failed miserably, even though a wrong report let it known that they had permitted the capture of Riencourt, then Hendecourt, whereas not a single tank, or even a single Australian infantryman, was seen in either village on 11 April. Most of the tanks had got bogged or burnt down and only two out of twelve were able to go back to their lines.

Admittedly, they had drawn enemy fire away from the infantry, but they were not able to break through the wire. Furthermore, in order to benefit from surprise, the plan had made no provisions for direct artillery support. As a consequence the Australians rushed on their own at the Hindenburg line where it was deepest. History shows few examples of an attack launched in such unfavourable conditions. Yet it succeeded. The wire had been destroyed more thoroughly than was thought by the previous days' shelling, and the Australians were able to capture the first German line.

◀ A second line Canadian
trench in front of Bullecourt.

**The men are cooking a meal
on a small stove. The weather
was particularly poor on April 11.
After taking the first German line,
then the second at the cost of of
very heavy losses, the Australians
were not able to continue towards
Riencourt and Bullecourt.**
(IWM)

A Stokes mortar and
its crew in a captured position.

**The mortar has been covered
with a tarpaulin. On the left
the crew are stacking shells.
After they took the first two lines,
the Australians were blocked
on the Hindenburg line, with no
other choice than to wait for
reinforcements which could not
get across no-man's-land
because of machine gun fire.
The two brigades were moreover
cut off from each other.
The Australians couldn't
hold until nightfall unless
they received powerful
artillery support.**
(IWM)

▶

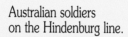

Australian soldiers   ▶
on the Hindenburg line.

**Because of the wrong report about
the tanks entering Riencourt,
the artillery commanding officer
refused to aim a barrage shelling
at a position just behind the
second German line. The British
command's optimism was shared
by Gough, who even ordered the
4th Cavalry Division to move
forward. The cavalry was to be
scattered by machine gun
and artillery fire.** *(IWM)*

A view of the battlefield.   ▼

**This photograph is more significant
than it looks, as it shows what
impossible task lay ahead for
the Australians: advancing on
open ground on this terrain
with no artillery support.** *(IWM)*

Australian soldiers on the
eve of the battle of Bullecourt. ▶

The Australians were excellent
soldiers, which probably explains
why Gough decided to launch them
into the battle in such unfavourable
conditions. However the Australian
C.O., general Birdwood, would not
be convinced. He doubted that it
was wise to attack and thought a
victory could only be obtained
under two conditions: massive
tank support and the Third Army
breaking through he German front.
Gough's chief-of-staff, after
consulting with the latter, answered
that the attack would be launched
anyway. Some time later, another
high-ranking Australian officer,
White, asked again that the attack
be delayed. The latest reports had
shown that the Third Army's right
wing had been stopped before the
Hindenburg line. Gough cynically
replied that this gave a further
reason for attempting something
on the Fifth Army's front.
The suicide attack was
accordingly launched. *(IWM)*

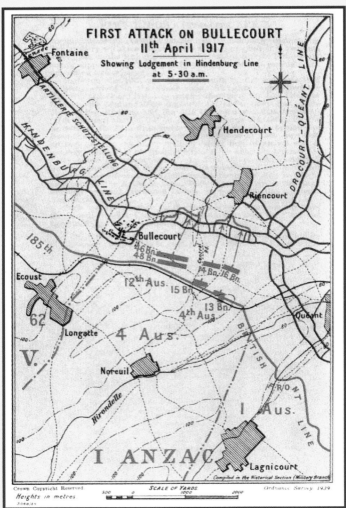

A map of the Bullecourt sector.

The Australians were to attack
inside a pocket, under enfilade fire
from two sides at the same time.
Troops from Britain would not have
been sacrificed in this way.
(British Official History) ▶

◄ An Australian
armoured car opens fire
on a German aeroplane.

This second view of the terrain
before Bullecourt gives evidence
that there were no shelters
for the infantry apart from shell
holes and trenches. The return of
the 4th Brigade across
no-man's-land completed the
unit's destruction, with the loss
of 2,258 out of its 3,000 men
in a single morning. The
12th Australian Brigade suffered
somewhat less, but still lost
909 men. The Germans captured
27 officers and 1,137 men,
a high number explained by the
lack of ammunition for the
isolated Australians. German
losses amounted to 750 men.
(IWM)

A captured German trench.

The 48th Battalion became completely cut off in the Hindenburg
line after the 46th was destroyed,
but still continued to fight all
morning, not even aware it was
surrounded. Running short of
ammunition and caught under the
fire of the British artillery that
had finally started firing, but on
the wrong target, the battalion
▼ managed an orderly retreat.
(IWM)

A house destroyed by the Germans in Bapaume. ▶

After the failure of his first offensive at Bullecourt, general Gough ordered fresh preparations. The rear of the Fifth Army was thus very busy, while their work was made more difficult by the German destructions in March. This house was blown up from the inside with explosives. An Australian supply cart is seen riding past.
(IWM)

Horror at Bullecourt

An Australian soldier asleep in a first line dug-out.

More troops were sent into the battle than before: there were six infantry brigades, that is to say two divisions, the 62nd and 2nd Australian, the former attacking west of Bullecourt, the latter east. ▼
(IWM)

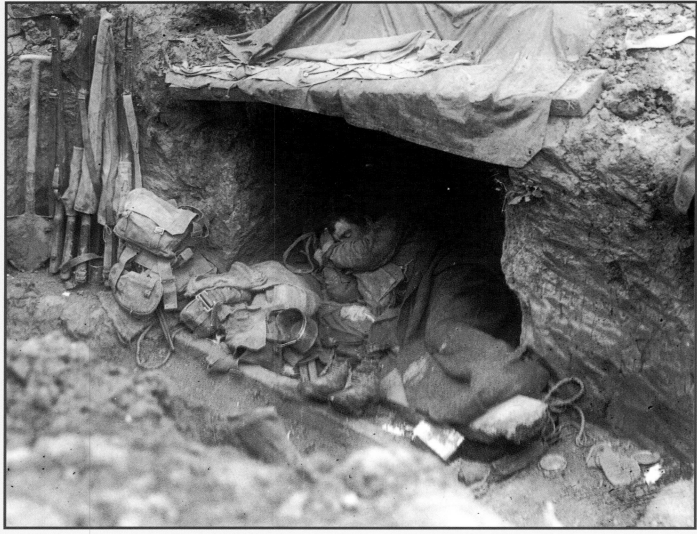

◀ General Birdwood, general Newton-Moore and captain Churnside are riding through the village of Grevillers in May 1917.

The attack was launched on May 3 1917 with the 2nd Australian Division advancing behind creeping fire and with the support of 96 machine guns. The 5th Brigade was pushed back by enfilade fire, but the 2nd got a foothold in the Hindenburg line where there ensued a terrible grenade fight. On the 62nd Division's front, all three brigades were hacked down and could not secure Bullecourt. Although it had thrown in all its battalions and lost 3,000 men, the division could not make a dent into the Hindenburg line.
(IWM)

Australian troops on the move on a narrow gauge track.

The battle raged on for fourteen days, with neither side taking a clear advantage. Eventually the village of Bullecourt was taken, but no breach had been made in the Hindenburg line. ▼
(IWM)

4th Australian
Division infantry on
the move in May 1917.

**The scene is more evocative
of a convoy setting out for the
bush - or maybe the Wild West -
than of the Great War. After two
weeks of battle at Bullecourt, the
Australians had lost 292 officers
and 7,190 men, and the British
300 officers and 6,500 men,
which adds up to more than
14,000 men - or 1,000 a day -
for meagre results.**
(IWM)

The end at Bullecourt

An Australian Vickers
crew on the move.

**The Australians' sacrifice at
Bullecourt, which came after
Fromelles in 1916, was to leave
deep wounds in Australian minds.
It is no wonder that conscription
was abolished in that country.**
(IWM)

◄ A GHQ car crossing the former German f ront line at Vimy.

From 10 to 12 April, the Canadian front was quiet: only the artillery started to redeploy in view of a possible new assault. Meanwhile the Germans were retreating to the Oppy-Méricourt line. The Canadians were able, in the following days, to take the villages of Givenchy, Vimy and Petit-Vimy, Farbus and Willerval. Bailleul, further west, was taken by the XII. British Corps. The only operation of some importance launched by the First Army consisted in the capture of Arleux and Oppy.
(IWM)

Heavy German howitzers captured at the foot of the Vimy ridge.

The British failed in front of Oppy, but the Canadian corps launched a determined attack against Arleux and secured the village after two days of fighting, on 28-29 April. This signalled the end of the batle of Arras on the front of the First Army. It had lost about 24,000 men in the fights, while taking 5,784 prisoners, 69 guns and, more importantly, the formidable position at Vimy. But it had never been in a position to achieve a decisive breakthrough. ▼
(IWM)

Red tape found its way into the trenches.

The picture was taken near Guémappes on 29 April 1917. It shows men of the City of London Regiment (Royal Fusiliers). After Monchy-le-Preux was captured, the Third Army's offensive lost some of its punch for the reasons mentioned earlier. The next three days saw numerous British attempts which lacked coordination and had no tangible results, but cost many lives. The trench warfare was resumed, yet Haig did not want to stop his offensive, first because Nivelle was about to launch his attack and also because Haig still believed he could force a victory. *(IWM)*

German prisoners leaving Arras to bring back corpses.

After their first failure at Bullecourt, the British attacked again on both sides of the Scarpe, on 23-24 April, again on 27-28 April, and finally on 3-4 May 1917. The gains were negligible. In April the British army lost 104,862 men. *(IWM)*

The end of the battle of Arras

◄ An Fe 2 captured in April 1917 and a Sopwith Pup wrecked on landing.

One may not conclude on the battle of Arras without a mention of the fights that took place in the skies of Pas-de-Calais, known as Bloody April to the Royal Flying Corps. Historians still argue as to which side obtained air supremacy in that period. This writer tends to favour the version given by British official history: namely, that the Royal Flying Corps and the RNAS (Royal Naval Air Service) controlled the air at the time of the offensive, but only at the cost of terrible losses, far superior to the Germans'. A count made after the war matching the records of both countries yields this comparison:

● British losses:
  - 151 aircraft;
  - 316 airmen either killed or missing.

● German losses:
  - 66 aircraft;
  - 119 airmen killed or missing.

British losses were thus almost twice as heavy as the enemy's. The Albatros DIII was better than any British plane except the new Bristol Fighter, which was not used adequately. But it is clear that in spite of Britain's technical inferiority in aircraft and even pilots, missions were always carried out with the greatest courage, even though losses were substantial. This explains how mastery of the sky could be obtained above the battlefield, whatever the cost.
(Bundesarchiv and MAP)

An overturned Albatros after an emergency landing.

In spite of their numerous victories in the air, the Germans were outnumbered and preferred not to venture above the British lines. This is why the preparations of the First and Third Armies were never spotted, or rather ill-interpreted: Allenby was thus to benefit from a clear advantage. Similarly, British planes outnumbered German planes above the battlefield proper. Their many missions included attacking the enemy Drachen, air reconnaissance, artillery cooperation, bombardment and even strafing the Hindenburg line trenches. It is no wonder that losses were severe.
(MAP) ►

The French plan and general Nivelle's forces

AS discussed in the introduction to chapter 1, general Nivelle's plan was built on the series of achievements obtained at Verdun in late 1916. Renewing this on a front that was ten times wider did not bother Nivelle, as he thought it was only a matter of increasing his forces tenfold. The success of the operation was based on three simple - not to say simplistic - elements, and the choice of terrain appeared inconsequential. The three elements were: surprise, rude force and swiftness. So persuaded was Nivelle of their efficiency that he simply ignored the terrain layout and the German defenses. If the artillery could destroy everything, the infantry would be able to climb the steep slopes of Chemin des Dames and ram into the German front.

In order to break through the enemy lines, a group of reserve armies was brought together under general Micheler's command. It included the 5ᵉ Armée (general Mazel), the 6ᵉ Armée (general Mangin) and the 10ᵉ Armée of general Duchêne. Those generals who did not share Nivelle's conceptions were removed, as was the case with Foch and de Castelnau.

Mangin's 6ᵉ Armée was to knock down the left wing of the front, between Chavonne and Heurtebise, and the 5ᵉ the right wing between Heurtebise and Rheims. This done, both armies would spread out while the 10ᵉ Armée was to charge straight ahead. Before the assault, the British offensive on the Scarpe would keep German reserves busy in the north, as would a French mock-attack at Saint-Quentin. If both the British at Arras and the French on the river Aisne should break the front, success would be complete. And even if the British failed, the French breakthrough would be enough to cause a general German retreat.

General Micheler informed his officers that he thought the front would be broken as early as D day, or in the morning of D + 1. So optimistic was Mangin that he himself set the pace of the infantry to a hundred metres per minute, a totally absurd proposition if one remembers that army regulations specified a pace of 240 meters per three minutes on a peaceful road and under ordinary conditions. Mangin wrote in his orders: "*By dawn of the second day the cavalry should ride onto the plain of*

Laon and the infantry should occupy the Laon-Lanicourt-Anizy-le-Château line". By D + 4, the town of Saint-Quentin should be reached. Micheler was more cautious and reminded Mangin that the artillery had to be able to keep up, while the infantry could not be expected to advance all day at the pace of 100 meters per minute. Nivelle did not back either general: his opinion was that every division was to rush ahead until it had reached the end of its offensive capacity, but he was well aware that Mangin's plan was unlikely to be fully carried out. That being said, he persisted: "*I insist on the violence, brutality and swiftness of our offensive and most particularly on its first stage, breaking up the front, with the immediate targets of capturing the enemy positions and the whole area of its artillery*".

Every officer who was part of the plan shared Nivelle's enthusiasm, at least among army commanders. In lower ranks there was some doubt. Thus colonel Messimy, who had been war minister and now commanded a division's infantry, noted: "*At the cost of the greatest sacrifice we may gain 10 or 20 kilometers with no strategically significant result, and we will be stopped by the German reserves*". The generals who had been kept aside also voiced their worries. Pétain for example warned that "*General Nivelle's obstinacy will lead to failure. (...). It is fanciful to think that the second line will be crossed. With a carefully prepared attack and fair weather, it could be taken, but not easily. An offensive is needed, but it should be limited to short-range, well-defined attacks*". These doubts led war minister Painlevé to call a summit meeting.

This took place in Compiègne and was chaired by president Poincaré. Some generals, among them Pétain, confronted Nivelle. The commander-in-chief stated that if the assault failed to break through the front he would not persist and would call it off after 48 hours. It would not go on for twenty weeks as on the Somme. But Nivelle eventually lost his temper at the generals' and ministers' questions, and offered to resign. This was certainly going too far for the politicians, who had just replaced Joffre and could not disown themselves. Nivelle was accordingly confirmed in his position.The worries that prevailed in some political and military circles were largely unknown to the poilus. Most believed in a

◀ The infantry of Chemin
des Dames going into the battle.

**This was lieutenant Pochard's
company, of 132e RI.**
(photo by Pochard, Vautillier collection)

The crew of a
Chauchat light machine gun. ▶

**The Chauchat light machine gun,
also known as FM modèle 1915,
only appeared in the course of the
year 1916, mostly in the second
half. It was used in the battles of
Verdun and the Somme, but the
Chemin des Dames offensive was the
first for which all infantry units had
been supplied with it. It was no
miracle weapon by far and had many
faults, some due to low construction
standards and others to errors of
design. It jammed easily on muddy
terrain and its practical range was
poor. However it provided the
infantry with a firepower it did not
have before. Also called CSRG
after the names of its designers
(Chauchat, Sutter, Ribeyrolles and
Gladiator), the FM modèle 1915 was
first and foremost a weapon born
of the circumstances.**
(Author's collection)

General Nivelle in early 1917.

**He was not a young man, having
just turned 60, but his star had
been shining for a few months only
and he had such faith in theory
that he was able to impose himself
as Joffre's successor.**
(Archipel/BDIC) ▼

major, if not decisive, victory. Noblécourt quotes extracts from soldiers' letters in his excellent book « *Les Fantassins du Chemin des Dames* »: "*I don't know what they have in store for us, but the preparations are huge. Troops and ammunition keep pouring in. If they could at least wait until I have returned from leave*"; "You'll be staggered when you see the results of the big offensive"; "The great victory will come soon. The Boches are on their last leg, they're starving. Believe me, you'll hear of great things before long".

Some were less enthusiastic, though: "*Haven't we suffered enough yet? Are more slaughters needed? This already gets me down*"; "*The end will not come within two months as some imagine. I think that if we are still alive one year from now, we won't have got any further than today. If the offensive is launched, that's 500,000 dead men*". The most significant letter is probably this: "*Christ, what a job it is to be in the infantry! I'm not sure the enemy will give up the terrain we are considering taking from them. If not, we're going to have a hell of a time*".

Hope was great, huge even, but it might be matched by equal disappointment. The news of the German retreat had strengthened the poilu's opinion that victory was at hand. Still, there were some who feared it might be a trap, as they knew their adversary and could judge their worth as fighters, contrary to what the press wrote. Was morale at its highest on the eve of the attack, then? On the whole, the answer is yes, although it had definitely sagged in the winter of 1916-1917. The men had then complained of the food, lack of leaves, clothing and fatigues. The carelessness and disregard of those in command had been questioned. Nivelle may have had his shortcomings – particularly an astounding self-confidence bordering on stubbornness – but he was no fool, far from it. On 8 March, he sent his officers the interesting instruction that they were to "convince themselves of the idea that efficiency in battle is always in proportion to the moral and material care provided by the leaders".

On the eve of the attack of 16 April, confidence had returned, maybe on the surface only, yet very clearly on the face of the unbelievable profusion of equipment and ammunition prepared for the offensive.

A 155-mm gun in Loivre.

This was one of the new Schneider guns, capable of firing a 45-kg shell at a target 13 miles away. General Nivelle could use really impressive artillery forces for his offensive. It seems that the exact number is not known down to a unit, but French official history, "*les Armées Françaises dans la Grande Guerre*", gives this breakdown on 16 April 1917:
- **2,900 field guns;**
- **1,650 heavy guns;**
- **160 long-range heavy guns (ALGP);**
- **1,550 trench mortars.**

In addition Britain had lent 24 150-mm howitzers. Without taking them into the count, there was a total of 5,360 guns spread out on the fronts of 6e and 5e Armées.
(Archipel/BDIC)

Widening the road to Berry-au-Bac, at Cormicy, in January 1917.

In the months before their offensive the French made thorough preparations. Nivelle was a good organizer who left nothing to chance, in order that the artillery might make use of its full power.
(Archipel/BDIC) ▼

Massive preparations

Unlimbering a
240-mm mortar at Beaurieux. ▲

The two front wheels are being
removed. Nivelle was an artillery
man and his whole theory was
based on the proper use of
ordnance. The French industry
was now in full production and
could hope to beat the Germans
on their own ground, all the more
as the Entente had unlimited
supplies of raw materials. On the
attack front there was one heavy
gun every 21 yards and one field
gun or trench mortar every
23 yards. Never before had
such artillery concentration
been seen in a French offensive.
(Archipel/BDIC)

Inflating a "saucisse",
or observation balloon.

The photo was certainly taken
well away from the front as no
man is seen wearing the Adrian
helmet. Observation of the
German lines was necessary to
direct the artillery efficiently.
This could be achieved by means
of the saucisses or artillery
cooperation aircraft, but the
German air force was found
very aggressive, to the point
of "insolence".
(BDIC)

▶

Training on a 37-mm gun. ▶

This gun appeared of little use in trench warfare, but two notes from general Nivelle dated from early 1917 insisted on its role in anti-tank defense. While there was no indication that the Germans did have tanks, the French commander-in-chief prefered to make the first move. Also, he ordered the construction of 2,500 tanks in March 1917. *(IWM)*

The artillery, queen of battles

▲ A field artillery battery
en route to the front.

The 75-mm gun was the main,
if not only, gun of the field artillery. Older models were still in use,
although less and less. It is worth
noting that while the French
artillery concentration was
unprecedented, its power was
not higher than on the Somme,
but lower. The explanation is that
the targets were no longer
restricted to the first and second
lines, but now included the third
and fourth as well. And the latter
two could only be hit by heavy
artillery, although all guns
had been placed as close as
reasonable to the enemy
trenches. German counter-
battery fire would be all
the more damaging.
(IWM)

A bogged down
old Bange system gun.

By April 1917, most of these
old slow-firing units had
been replaced by the
155-mm Schneider gun, a
much more efficient weapon.
From 8 April the artillery
was used to open breaches
in the wire lines. A firing
record from a battery of the
10e Division Coloniale gives
an indication of the rate of
fire on specific targets: one
shot every nine minutes on
9 April, but a huge 1,209 shells
for two breaches on 14 April.
(IWM)

A 240-mm gun firing in Beaurieux.

The chief difference between previous French attacks and Chemin des Dames lay in the importance of heavy artillery. In the first years of the war, the 75-mm guns had to carry out, for better or for worse, all the artillery's tasks. In 1917 this was no longer true. *(Archipel/BDIC)*

"Nénette" was a 155-mm Schneider gun in position at Beaurieux.

This belonged to captain Grisot's battery. The artillery attack began on 2 April with what was called discrete ranging, then went on until 11 April with destruction and counter-battery fire. The two consecutive delays of 11-14 April and 14-16 April increased the ammunition consumption alarmingly. But the poilus were overjoyed at the avalanche of fire hitting the Germans. This was a somewhat distorted view however, as the French shelling may have badly damaged the first line, but much less the ones behind.
(Archipel/BDIC)

An army of infantry under the command of non-infantry men

A trench mortar shell dump in Cormicy, early 1917.

These were the celebrated Crapouillots. With 1,550 guns of this type lined up on the attack front, the 6e and 5e Armées had the means to level out the first German line and its wire. Beyond that, their range was too short.
(Archipel/BDIC)

◄ A 75-mm gun firing in Beaulne and Chivy, April 1917.

A major paradox of the French army in the first three years of the Great War must be noted: although composed of 90% infantry fighting an infantry war, it was not under the command of generals from the infantry. Joffre for example was from the Engineers, Nivelle from the artillery. Naturally both Engineers and artillery played a great role in the trench war, but it is an infantry general, Pétain, who first understood that "fire kills", an obvious fact that was totally ignored by non-infantry officers.
(Archipel/BDIC)

▼ A 155-mm Schneider battery near Cormicy.

The German counter-battery fire was efficient: at the end of the preparation shelling on the 6e corps' front, out of 100 guns of this calibre 27 had gone, and only 75,000 155-mm shots could be fired instead of the planned 111,000.
(BDCI/Archipel)

"Patte de Velours" and *"Pourquoi Pas"*, two Schneider tanks photographed near Courlandon before the battle.

The available tanks were placed under the 5e armée, which had two groups of unequal size, both made up of Schneider tanks as the Saint-Chamond was running into adjustment problems and was not operational.
The Chaubes group was to support the 5e corps d'armée. It was made up of three teams of 16 Schneider tanks each, plus a repair and supply unit. The Bossut group was to help the 32e corps' offensive. It had five teams of 16 tanks and a repair unit. Altogether there were 128 tanks, which were delivered on 10 April at Ventelay and Courlandon, from where they moved to a standby position at Cuiry-les-Chaudardes. This was the first French tank attack, and it is worth noting that never before had so many tanks been used on the same day.
(BDIC/Archipel)

Nivelle believed in tanks and planes

N. 1079 La Noblette (Marne)
Départ d'une patrouille d'avions de chasse.
Avril 17

At La Noblette, in the Marne ▲
département, a flight of Nieuport
17s is ready for takeoff.

The photo is interesting as it
shows different versions of the
aircraft. The one in the middle
is equipped with a large propeller
boss, which was uncommon but
not an exception with
Nieuport 17s. The armament
includes a synchronized machine
gun shooting through the propeller arc and one or two weapons
placed on the upper wing,
shooting over this arc.
The picture does not permit
further identification of these.
(Archipel/BDIC)

General Maistre is reviewing
a squadron of Spad VIIs
at the time of the Chemin
des Dames offensive.

The French air force in the sector
of GAR had 500 reconnaissance
and artillery cooperation aircraft,
i.e. 19 from the 5e armée,
16 from the 6e armée, 8 from
the 10e armée and 4 from the
long-range heavy artillery,
for a total of 47 squadrons.
There were fewer fighters: only
13 squadrons, 4 of which were
missing on 7 April. And half
of the aircraft were not
operational.
(BDIC/Archipel)

A 155-mm gun
in Soupir, early April.

The weather was so bad in
early April that the offensive
was postponed twice. The
artillery sometimes had to
operate in dreadful conditions,
as in this flooded pit.
Official records note: *"Weather
conditions have not improved
and almost every day air and
ground observation have been
difficult, if not impossible"*.
On 13 April the general
commanding the 41e division
wrote: *"It is urgent to give the
artillery the means to do its job
if the front is to be broken on
D day. More planes! More
ammunition!"* The roads
were broken up.
(BDCI/Archipel)

The end of
the artillery
preparation

▲ 155-mm guns in the heat of action near Cormicy.

The artillery preparation went on for two weeks instead of ten days, but battalion C.O. Nicolas wrote in a report dated 14 April: *"The preparation is not what was hoped. There are gaps, so that the infantry will face strong resistance. They will find half-open breaches and repaired breaches. The enemy is repairing up to their first positions and our interdiction fire cannot stop them (...). The 1er corps d'armée is intent on getting through, but it will cost dearly. Everyone's feeling is that it will be a difficult battle, but everyone is getting ready with cold determination".*
(BDIC/Archipel)

A view of Craonne and the Californie plateau.

The picture was taken on **7 May** and not **16 April**, that is to say after more than three weeks of intense shelling. On the eve of the assault general Mangin summarized on the destructions: *"1st position, wholly; 2nd position, partly, sufficient preparation, yet showing only in places the characteristic aspect of the upheavals of the Somme or Verdun; everywhere else, scattered damage, and few demolitions".*
(BDIC/Archipel)

The German army's countering measures

THE first condition to the success of the French attack was the surprise effect. And yet, rarely had a secret been kept so poorly. Nobécourt called it an open secret. In his memoirs, Ludendorff wrote that during a raid at la Main de Massiges, German soldiers found an order from the 2e D.I., dated 29 January, concerning a planned attack on the river Aisne. Ludendorff's conclusion: "*This was a capital piece of information*". The French army's historical department has never found any trace of the order in the records, but this is no evidence that it never existed. The Germans received a further hint from a raid carried out on 3 March 1917 by the 51. R.I.D. which, as the Kronprinz wrote, "*brought us into possession of the French regulation document known as Instructions concerning the aim and conditions of a general offensive. This had been implemented by Nivelle on 16 December 1917. It contained highly invaluable information. It made it clear that this time it would not be an attack on a specific target but a sweeping breakthrough offensive*". This allowed the Germans to take preventive steps. Late in March, a second lieutenant of the artillery went missing with documented maps during a reconnaissance mission. Even more seriously, the Germans launched a limited attack between Loivre and Berry-au-Bac on 4 April and got hold of the battle plan for 3e zouaves and 37e D.I. as well as the planned movements of 7e, 32e and 38e corps and the objectives north of the Aisne - in short the whole French plan, which was immediately passed on to German headquarters. As a matter of fact, German prisoners captured on 16 April said that they knew the date and even the time of the French attack. In Parisian political circles everyone had known for months where the attack would be launched. Jean de Pierrefeu writes that at GQG everybody was talking about it: "*No one had bothered to keep the date of the offensive secret. It was an open*

subject. I am still wondering why in the circumstances everyone was so talkative. It was learnt that the attack had been postponed because of continuing bad weather, that the destructions were not completed. The batmen themselves were asking about the weather forecast and looked up at the sky with worried faces. This really was the first time that a planned offensive was discussed so openly".

Ludendorff acted quickly. In January, the Germans reportedly had four divisions facing the 6e armée. Just before the battle the number had risen to seven, or more likely eight divisions, a 100% increase east of Vailly. Likewise for the artillery, where the number of known batteries increased by over 100% all over the front and heavy guns were brought in. There were six batteries per kilometre. The air force and the number of Drachen had similarly been strengthened.

Nobécourt gives this description of the German lines: «*Three positions, sometimes four, with at least two lines each, spread a deep network over the terrain. The older trenches, around Chemin des Dames, had been reorganized with support positions flanked by blockhaus placed at intervals covering every inch of the ground with their machine guns. On the plain east of the bluff as well as on top of the bluff itself and on its slope (...), the Germans had dug out spacious galleries, which backed up and served the whole system.*»

In front of the 5e armée the Germans had strengthened their positions in the same way: the five known divisions of 15 February had become nine or ten by 15 April. The artillery reinforcement was even stronger: 53 active batteries on 1 March, 392 on 15 April! Most seriously, in the Laon-Rethel-Pont-Faverger sector behind the front were at least 12, maybe 15 divisions ready for a sudden attack. Should a first line division yield, Ludendorff had plans for the immediate intervention of reserve divisions.

▼ Watching the French lines
from Chemin des Dames.

**The shelling could not destroy
the deeper shelters.**
(Bundesarchiv)

▲ A 17-cm Minenwerfer
capable of firing explosive or gas shells.

**The wheels made it possible to move
this heavy piece around fairly easily.**
(IWM)

Unusually, this MG 08 machine gun has been set up on top of a tree trunk.

Facing the 6e armée the Germans had the following units:
❏ 23. Armee Korps:
- 13. Landwehr Division between Coucy-la-Ville and Brancourt;
- 211. Infanterie Division, between the canal and Laffaux;
- 222. Infanterie Division, between Laffaux and Condé-sur-Aisne;
❏ 11. Armee Korps:
- 25. Landwehr Division, between Condé-sur-Aisne and Chavonne;
- 183. Infanterie Division between Chavonne and Chivy;
- 16. Reserve Division between Chivy and Ailly.
❏ Gruppe Höhm:
- 5. Garde Division, between Ailly and northeast of Craonnelle. The latter was exceptionally good, while the former were average units, to the exception of the 16. Reserve Division which was first-rate too.
(BA)

A 77-mm gun firing, most likely on a practice rance.

The reinforcement of German defenses was known to the French high command, with frequent reminders from the enemy artillery. Thus on 15 April at 4 p.m. the 6e armée noted: "*German artillery of all calibres (105, 150 and 210) has taken the opportunity to fire vigorously at our positions, the first lines mainly*".
(IWM)

An artillery train riding up to the front.

Both men and horses are wearing gas masks. However the scene looks too quiet to warrant the use of this equipment and it was probably arranged for the photographer. On the other hand, troop and vehicle movements were very real in the weeks before the offensive. The following can be read in *Les Armées Françaises dans la Grande Guerre*: *"The reinforcement of the enemy, alert and watching, the strength of their defense system, the failings of the artillery preparation, the bad weather, the difficult movements on a broken up, shelled and muddy ground were so many factors that ran contrary to the GAR's offensive".*
(IWM)

The German divisions at Chemin des Dames

Widening a road in the German hinterland.

Ludendorff expected a powerful blow from the French and did everything to enable the reserve divisions to stop the tiniest breach as early as possible. He knew Nivelle would not have the means for a second attack.
(BA)

◄ Two views of German
shelters at Berry-au-Bac. ▲

**The leftmost picture is
particularly striking with
galleries dug out or rebuilt
by the Germans, which could
withstand the heaviest blows.
On the 5e armée front, the
German system was as follows:**
❑ **Gruppe Höhm:**
**- 5. Bayerische Division between
Choléra and Berry-au-Bac;**
❑ **Gruppe Eberhardt:**
**- 10. Reserve Division between
Berry-au-Bac and Godat;**
**- 21. Infanterie Division between
Godat and Loivre;**
**- 43. Reserve Division between
Loivre and Cavaliers de Courcy;**
**- 34. Infanterie Division between
Cavaliers de Courcy and Bétheny.**
❑ **7. Reserve Korps:**
**- 223. Infanterie Division between
Bétheny and Cernay;**
**- 13. Reserve Division between
Cernay and la Bertonnerie;**
**- 14. Reserve Division between la
Bertonnerie and les Marquises;**
**- 214. Infanterie Division at les
Marquises.**
(Bundesarchiv)

An observation post
at Chemin des Dames.

**French preparations
were watched every day.**
(Bundesarchiv) ►

Ludendorff's intervention divisions are training
for open field combat in case the front should cave in.

Fall-back positions were set up everywhere behind the front: the
fights at Verdun in late 1915 had shown that the Allies were capable
of breaking through the front but could probably not capitalize on their
success if confronted by a mobile, clever enemy. Developments in the
battle of Arras after the British victory of 9 April gave confirmation of this.
(BA)

The German rear lines were shelled too.

We have insisted on the incomplete artillery preparation of the French, due to the fact that the many guns had been assigned multiple targets. However the shelling still had significant results. After four days of pounding, Albert Reichel, a Bavarian gunner, wrote: "*It is almost impossible to identify the trenches now, one crater joins the next. We leave the shelter of our hut for the gun bunker; there at least we feel relatively safe. We have hardly got there when we are hit by a series of shells (...). The next blow pierces through the graveyard wall and end its course against our 30-cm thick concrete wall, which resists perfectly well. But under the terrible shock everything inside is turned upside down and scattered around, a heavy table is thrown aside and a bench lands on top of it, wrong side up. Around the bunker nothing looks familiar. We are totally stunned, our skulls are shattered*".
(Bundesarchiv)

The Germans are ready

An MG 08 machine gun
in a shallow trench. ▲

**The MG O8 mount was bulky
and not adapted to trench use.
Here it has been removed and
replaced by a less cumbersome
board. Like everywhere else
since the beginning of the war,
the Germans counted on their
machine guns to stop the
French infantry.**
(BA)

Using a rangefinder,
German observers are trying
to locate the French batteries. ▶

**The higher position of the
German batteries was an
incomparable advantage.
In spite of the care taken by
the French before the offensive,
their preparations did not go
unnoticed and German shelling
made it more difficult to bring
in ammunition.** *(BA)*

◀ Loading a heavy gun.

**Judging from the diameter
of the shell, this is a piece of
a huge calibre, 300 mm at least.
The shell is loaded with the
help of a cart, then six men
slide it into the breech.
The Germans used conventional
explosive shells, but also gas
shells. These were less efficient,
but still slowed down the
enemy gunners as they were
obliged to wear masks.**
(IWM)

A field dressing station
in the second or third line. ▲

The mess tin on the right
was used to sound gas alerts.
As every step had been taken to
repel the coming assault, German
troops felt fairly confident.
On 11 April general von Liebert
sent this order of the day to his
men holding the Vauclerc and
Californie plateaus: *"The time
has come for the decisive
combat. The strengthening of
the enemy fire tells of an
imminent assault on our
trenches. Our braves from
the Rhineland, Hanover and,
of course, the Garde regiments
will fight dearly for their
positions. I trust that not
one man will give himself up"*.
(Bundesarchiv)

Night before combat on the Aisne

Playing cards
in a ruined house.

The gunners are displaying both
their own weapon, a heavy MG
08, and a British Lewis light
machine gun without its round-
shaped magazine. These men
have certainly been on the British
front. Without its magazine and
ammo, their Lewis is a trophy
more than a usable weapon,.
▶
(Bundesarchiv)

Strong shelters have
been put up behind the front. ▲

**This one seems to have been used both
as a resting place and field dressing
station. The two vehicles are ambulances.
The men are ready to get into battle at
early notice.**
(BA)

A heavy piece of
ordnance on the move in the rear.

**The 17-cm gun is camouflaged
with diamond-shaped coloured
spots like German planes at
the time. The tractor is fitted
with solid wheels.**
(Bundesarchiv)

▼

The offensive on the 6ᵉ armée front

GENERAL Mangin's 6ᵉ armée lined up 37 infantry divisions organized in five corps, one cavalry division, the 5ᵉ and 97ᵉ division territoriale. Out of this total, eight infantry divisions were placed in first line (see table on next page). After the front had been broken, the 11ᵉ corps d'armée would join in the battle between the 20ᵉ corps and the 2ᵉ corps colonial, for the exploitation phase, between H + 4 and H + 6. Despite Mangin's requests, the 6ᵉ armée had no tank at its disposal.

During the night it rained and movements were made difficult by a very dark night and the poor condition of trenches. The attack started as planned at 6 a.m. on the 6ᵉ armée front, in cloudy and foggy weather. Observation of the advance was not easy, but it appeared that everything was not going according to plan. At the GQG, Nivelle and all the staff were waiting for news. Jean de Pierrefeu wrote: *"Hope was short-lived on 16 April. By 11 a.m. the 3ᵉ bureau had not yet sent any army reports, whereas in times of offensive telegrams would come in every hour after the beginning of the assault. This was not a good sign. Rain was pouring down, Compiègne was drowned in a violent storm, the barometre was low. I went to the 3ᵉ bureau. It was steeped in silence as on the darkest days. We didn't have enough information, I was told, but the first news was encouraging".*

In fact Nivelle only received the first news at 10:30 a.m. through a phone call from Gamelin, who was at the QG of the group of reserve armies in Savigny. Here is the report: *"Our information shows that the battle is taking place on the 1st and 2nd positions.*

The advance is particularly good in the sector of 5e CA, where air reconnaissance reports the arrival of the tanks in the vicinity of the Corbeny-Juvincourt front (...). Concerning the 6ᵉ armée, the right wing seems to have reached Ailles, region of la Bovelle, Cerny-en-Laonnais. Slower progress in the west, especially with corps Mitry (6e corps), where we only have the 1st line and backup trenches; Chavonne has been taken back from us; no news for the moment from corps Berdoulat, which must have attacked at 9 a.m".

One should not be surprised that Gamelin became general-chief-of-staff of the French armies in the next war: he showed remarkable diplomacy in announcing failure. His first sentence was terrible for Nivelle, although it was phrased casually: the battle is taking place on the 1st and 2nd positions. This was the exact opposite of what Nivelle had thought and hoped.

A view of Mont Sapin, west of Soupir.

It was photographed just after its capture. The entrance to a German dug-out can be seen on the left. The French lines were further down and the difficulty of the assault in a wood hacked to pieces by shells and machine guns is obvious.
(Archipel/BDIC)

Last letter from the trench.

On Sunday, April 15, unit COs were informed by a message delivered in a yellow envelope that D day was the next day, the 16th, and H hour 6 a.m. The soldiers were told. They prepared their kit, wrote a last letter, and, after mess time, went to sleep - or rather tried in spite of their anguish, although their morale was good. Morning call was at 3:30 a.m.
(BDIC/Archipel)

A French bugler killed during the assault at Moulin de Laffaux.

West of the 6ᵉ armée failure was complete, with most units thrown back to their starting positions.
(BDIC/Archipel)

Distribution of first line 6ᵉ armée forces

❑ **1er corps colonial :**

Between Vauxaillon and Laffaux
3ᵉ division coloniale (north)
2ᵉ division coloniale (south)
Attack towards Pinon

❑ **6ᵉ corps d'armée :**

On Soupir front, Metz farm
56ᵉ division d'infanterie (north)
127ᵉ division d'infanterie (south)
Attack towards Chavignon
6e corps covered by special Aisne detachment

❑ **20ᵉ corps :**

the Oise-Aisne canal and the sugarmill at Troyon
39ᵉ division d'infanterie (west)
153ᵉ division d'infanterie (east)
Attack towards Monampteuil

❑ **2ᵉ corps colonial :**

Between Troyon and Oulches
15ᵉ division coloniale (west)
10ᵉ division coloniale (east)
Attack via Vauclerc plateau towards the Martigny-Ployart wood line

The assault on Hurtebise farm

The farm in 1914, 1916 and 1917.

Napoleon is said to have taken a rest under the elms during his battle of 1814. This key location on Chemin des Dames remained under German control after the battle of the Marne. Very close to the lines, the farm was soon to become a ruin. On 16 April 1917 it was the scene of fierce fighting when the 2ᵉ corps colonial tried to take it. *(Archipel/BDCI)*

Watching the ridge
of Chemin des Dames
from the French lines.

The **2ᵉ corps colonial** came out
of their trenches without any
problem and reached the ridge
of Chemin des Dames between
7 and 8 a.m. General Marchand's
(a name associated with Fachoda)
10ᵉ DI had to climb up the
Foulon valley to storm
Hurtebise farm, then proceed
into the forest of Vauclerc, down
to the Ailette valley, across the
Bièvre valley and up a last line
of hills to finally see Laon and
its plain in the distance. It was
supposed to get there by H + 7.
In fact it did not go beyond the
farms of Hurtebise and Creute.
Apparently a battalion of 73ᵉ RIC
reached the vicinity of Ailles
before being surrounded and
destroyed there. Losses were
heavy, and the four colonels who
had led the Senegalese in the
assault were all killed but one.
Official history describes the
situation on the Hurtebise
isthmus in these words:
*"The two consecutive assault
waves that attacked at an
interval of thirty minutes
mingled with the remnants
of the foremost units and
suffered their heaviest
losses while retreating".*
As the creeping fire uselessly
continued to move on, the
brigadiers had it adjusted:
they first set it back to the
H+1:30 line, then back again
to the H + 0:30 line, which
gives a measure of the failure.
(Archipel/BDIC)

The 2ᵉ corps colonial
in the storm of Hurtebise

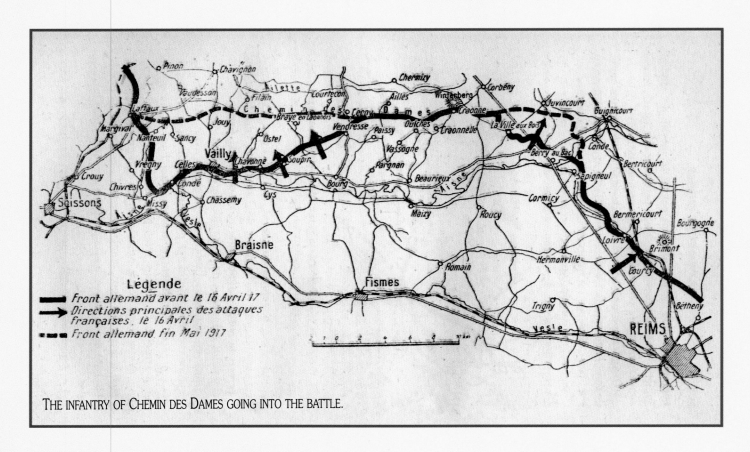

Légende

▬▬ *Front allemand avant le 16 Avril 17*
➤ *Directions principales des attaques
françaises, le 16 Avril*
▬ ▬ *Front allemand fin Mai 1917*

THE INFANTRY OF CHEMIN DES DAMES GOING INTO THE BATTLE.

In spite of the rain flooding their positions, the gunners fired on to support the infantry.

The readjustements in the barrage did not please general Mangin, who refused to face the truth. At 9:55 a.m. he gave this order: "*Resuming the preparation is a mistake. It shows that our infantry hesitates to move on. Our artillery preparation can't have left the enemy with the means to set up a solid line of machine guns. We must take advantage of gaps and outflank the resistance pockets*". Losses in 10e DI were so heavy that the troops obviously could no longer advance.
(BDIC)

A body deep in mud gives evidence of the fierceness of the fight.

A report from the division read: "*Most of the African battalions, weakened by the cold, rain and bivouac, have seriously impaired morale and might well panick at the least German attack, especially by night*". This shows how precariously the division and 15e DIC were holding the Hurtebise sector.
(BDIC)

Two views taken in captured German lines.

On the 20e corps' front, the attack began rather well. The 153e DI advanced quickly up to the sugarmill at Cerny and a regiment of Moroccan infantrymen reached the southern edge of Paradise wood, an inappropriate name for what looked more like hell: the Germans held on fiercely and progression was soon halted. To the left, the 39e DI moved on slowly and the artillery barrage was soon stopped, then readjusted. By 8:10 a.m. Mangin had realized that he had no breakthrough, but he still wanted to believe in success. Consequently he ordered the 20e corps: *"Carry out artillery barrage according to schedule. Try to catch up on delay. Also remind that points of resistance must be outflanked"*. In the light of the events of 16 April, his instructions about covering 100 meters in three minutes look laughable. The Moroccan regiment still reached into the second German line.
(BDIC/Archipel)
▶

The assault of 20^e and 6^e corps

Crapouillot shelling of Goutte d'Or wood on 14 April 1917.

On the left, facing Goutte d'Or wood, the wire was still standing in spite of trench artillery fire such as shown here. The infantry was stuck and at its request a new preparation was directed at the enemy wire lines. This angered general Mangin, who at 10:30 ordered: "*Unit Hellot must continue its progression. If the wire is not destroyed, have it cut by infantry; we must gain ground*". But the infantry remained pinned to the ground by machine guns and in spite of two attempts, in the afternoon and at 7 p.m., could not progress significantly.
(BDIC)

In the ruins of Soupir, 30 April 1917.

French soldiers are sorting out the ammo and weapons captured since 16 April. The 6^e corps made a promising start: it quickly passed the first line and the 56^e DI climbed up the slopes of la Bovette wood, then disappeared below the ridge, where they were met by a powerful machine gun barrage which checked their impetus.
(BDIC)

Two views of conquered German trenches at Mont sapin.

This is a rocky spur overlooking Soupir to the west. These trenches, occupied here by soldiers from Annam, are in excellent condition and have clearly not suffered much from the French artillery preparation. A report from the 127e DI shows what huge mistake Mangin had made when ordering the barrage to move 100 metres forward every three minutes: *"The main position to capture is Mont Sapin in the centre. The artillery barrage neutralizes the enemy's machine guns. The 25e BCP rushes at the Tirpitz trench, 30 prisoners, but the slope is almost vertical, the ground is broken up. The barrage moves 100 metres away in three minutes; very soon German machine guns materialize again and fire violently at the chasseurs (...). The second waves, in small detachments, join in and manoeuvre cleverly. The German grenadiers are subdued, the machine guns outflanked and captured in a fierce hand-to-hand fight, the minenwerfer servers are pinned down on their pieces. The capture of the caves of Mont Sapin gives us 300 prisoners including eight officers".* (BDIC/Archipel)

The fighting in front of Chavonne and Soupir

B. 5331. Aisne - Chavonne - Panorama. 30.4.17.

Chavonne. Auto-mitrailleuse contre avions. 30-4-17

Chavonne on 30 April 1917. ▲

The river Aisne winds its course at the foot of the hill. The destroyed bridge has been replaced by a floating bridge. While the chasseurs were holding the top of Mont Sapin against counter-attacks, the 335ᵉ RI entered into Chavonne. There a furious battle broke out, bombastically described by general d'Anselme, commanding officer of the DI: *"A fierce hand-to-hand combat erupts in the village. In a single cellar, one officer and 17 men are mopped out. (...). But during a violent counter-attack major Bruneau, who was constantly ahead of his battalion, disappears, either killed or wounded, the warrant officer is wounded next to the churchyard, the assault waves are stopped. Also, Chavonne no longer provides any cover: everything has been destroyed and the machine guns at les Grinons are sweeping all over the village, making it impossible to hold".*
(BDIC/Archipel)

Two Renault armoured cars in the ruins of Chavonne.

These machines were used for anti-aircraft defense and not for a breakthrough that did not take place. A German counter-attack recaptured most of Chavonne during the day, but the French clung on to a few houses on the west side and were still holding Mont Sapin and le Balcon. ▶
(BDIC/Archipel)

In a trench of the 132ᵉ RI. ▶

For the attack of 16 April, the regulation assault outfit was made slightly lighter. It included a tent section worn around the neck with a blanket rolled up inside, a two-litre waterbottle, an extra one-litre waterbottle, a gas mask, a trench spade, 120 Lebel cartridges, a haversack with personal belongings, a food haversack that was filled up by one loaf of bread, a strengthened bag with grenades (normally three hand grenades and two Vivien-Bessières rifle grenades) and finally a Lebel rifle. The haversacks and sand bag were left behind to make the soldiers lighter as they were to climb steep slopes.
(photo by Pochard, Vauvillier Collection)

The ruines chateau of Soupir.

Soupir stood very close to the German lines, almost on the front itself, but on the French side. The Germans controlled all the slopes overlooking the village and valley.
(Archipel/BDIC) ▼

Infantry pinned down on first enemy line

Map of the battlefield of Soupir and Chavonne.

It is not possible to understand the battle of Chemin des Dames without a relief map. The steep slopes were difficult to manage for heavily burdened infantrymen. This map showing the three German lines and the hills makes one wonder at the task demanded of the infantry. Lieutenant du Moncel left a remarkable description of what the officers on the field were thinking:
"There, between the two ink lines which define our sector, are exactly five lines of trenches that we must storm in one go: the Memel, Dresden, Brahms, Inglau and Kreutzer trenches; they are connected by a number of communication trenches; in-between are printed small crosses which represent wire lines, and small arrows - standing for machine guns - are pointing at every direction. The whole thing looks unprepossessing enough.... But probably nothing much of this remains? (...). We are to set off at H + 10 but only God knows when and where we will stop, for the regiment's objective is no less than Laon, over twenty kilometres north of our front". (SHAT)

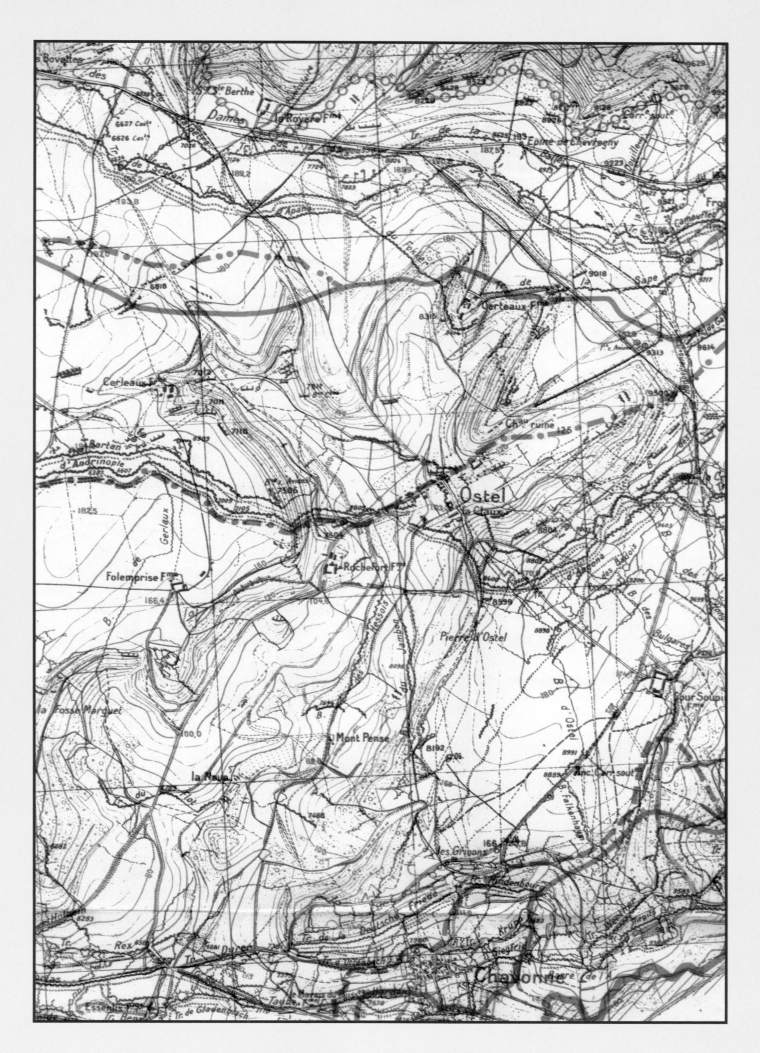

German prisoners captured in the Vauxaillon sector.

The date of the photo is not known, but it must be later than 16 April 1917, judging from the fact that the men appear to be hot. The capture of prisoners - and a small number at that - was the only tangible success on the front of the 1er corps colonial. The initial terrain gains were short-lived: Mont des Singes was occupied, partly thanks to the support of British artillery.
(Author's collection)

The defeat of the 1er corps colonial

A wounded man is evacuated before Laffaux.

Some troops, obeying general Mangin's orders, ignored their flanks and took advantage of a few breaches to advance up to the mill at Laffaux. Under fierce counter-attacks, they were driven back to their starting positions.
(BDIC/Archipel)

A French observer
is watching the enemy lines
through a periscope.

While the German artillery was
fairly quiet in the Laffaux sector,
their infantry was very aggressive
and deployed numerous machine
guns on open terrain in order
to mow down the French assault
waves. Losses were as high as
3,800 men in the 1[er] corps
colonial, while no German trench
of any significance could be kept:
Mont des Singes had to be
evacuated by its defenders as
the Germans were infiltrating
everywhere under cover of rain
or snow gales. The colonials still
clung halfway down the slope
and held two first-line trenches:
the Aviatik and Trous.
At 2 p.m., general Blondat
ordered a new artillery
preparation against the mill at
Laffaux, and a new attack was
launched four hours later, again
unsuccessfully because of the
German machine guns. The
reasons for the almost complete
defeat of 1[er] corps colonial are
mainly due to the time chosen for
the attack: 9 a.m., which was
almost three hours later than
elsewhere. No surprise effect
could be expected for this
flanking attack. The late time had
been chosen in order to avoid
that the 1[er] corps' troops, carried
on by their impetus, would arrive
too early in the Malmaison
redoubt ssector.
(BDIC/Archipel)

An ammunition
convoy at the rear.

Towards the end of the day,
it became obvious to general
Mangin that the breakthrough
had not been achieved anywhere.
And the few gains of the
6e armée still had to be kept.
As a consequence the artillery
was to increase their fire: "Very
strong interdiction fire will be
maintained day and night so as
to prevent the Germans from
relieving their troops or bring in
reserves". Mangin still ordered
the infantry to continue their
progression and capture the
whole of the Chemin des Dames
ridge, which they was well beyond
their capacity after the losses
of the day. (BDICArchipel)

April 16, 1917
on the front of the 5ᵉ armée

O N 16 April at 8 a.m. the GQG at Compiègne received a promising message from the staff of the 5ᵉ armée. It read: "*The infantry has made a very good start everywhere. Enemy barrage fire has usually been late and disorganized. At 7.30 a.m. intelligence informs us that the first enemy line has been taken all over the front. At one point, south of Juvincourt, it is reported that our troops have reached the second line*".

The war diary of the 5ᵉ armée reads: "*The infantry rushes into the battle. The enemy barrage is belated, weak and tentative. Everywhere, except in the centre of the 1ᵉʳ corps (1ʳᵉ DI) where the assault was immediately halted in front of the Balcon trench, our men have penetrated the enemy lines*".

At 10.30 a.m. Gamelin phoned the following report to Nivelle: "*The general idea of the front can be defined as follows, from right to left: Cavaliers de Courcy, Courcy, Loivre, Bermericourt, Champ du Seigneur, Sainte-Marie farm (these points included). - We have not recaptured mont Sapin yet. Situation undecided beyond mont Sapigneul and camp de César. We are in the batteries, just south of Juvincourt. Areas of Bois en T trench and l'Enclume wood ours. Fighting on Californie plateau*".

This was rather vague information, particularly concerning the most important piece: "*We are in the batteries, just south of Juvincourt*". Nivelle had always maintained that possession of the German battery lines would ensure a breakthrough. But Gamelin's wording was unprecise, and did not make it clear whether the batteries had actually been taken

A Schneider tank is leaving its camp at Courlandon for the Berry-au-Bac area. ▲

The only place where the second German line was reached and even passed was the Juvincourt sector, where the Bossut group of tanks attacked. It was the only success, even of a limited scope, on the first day of the offensive. This fine picture shows the Schneider's 75-mm gun and its low elevation. *(BDIC/Archipel)*

A map of the rightmost ▶ sector of the attacking front of 5ᵉ armée.

We can see here the sector of Brimont, Courcy, Loivre and Berméricourt, with the particularly deep first German line. *(Service historique de l'armée de terre map)*

or not. This lack of certainty was the only hope that the GQG could still hold to in the morning of 16 April, but it could not intervene to exploit the success. Jean de Pierrefeu, who wrote the communiqué, describes his call at 3ᵉ bureau: "*We lacked information, they said, but the first news were encouraging. I had heard all this before and entertained no hope of knowing exactly what had happened. At such times I would simply ask whether I should write a victory communiqué or remain more cautious, and what line I could say had been reached by our troops. But I was answered that it was better to wait until the evening commiqué to announce results, as those that were now known were still too vague*".

Indeed the morning communiqué released at 2 p.m. did not even mention the beginning of the great offensive. It simply noted: "*The artillery batlle has become extremely violent during the night over all the front between Soissons and Rheims*".

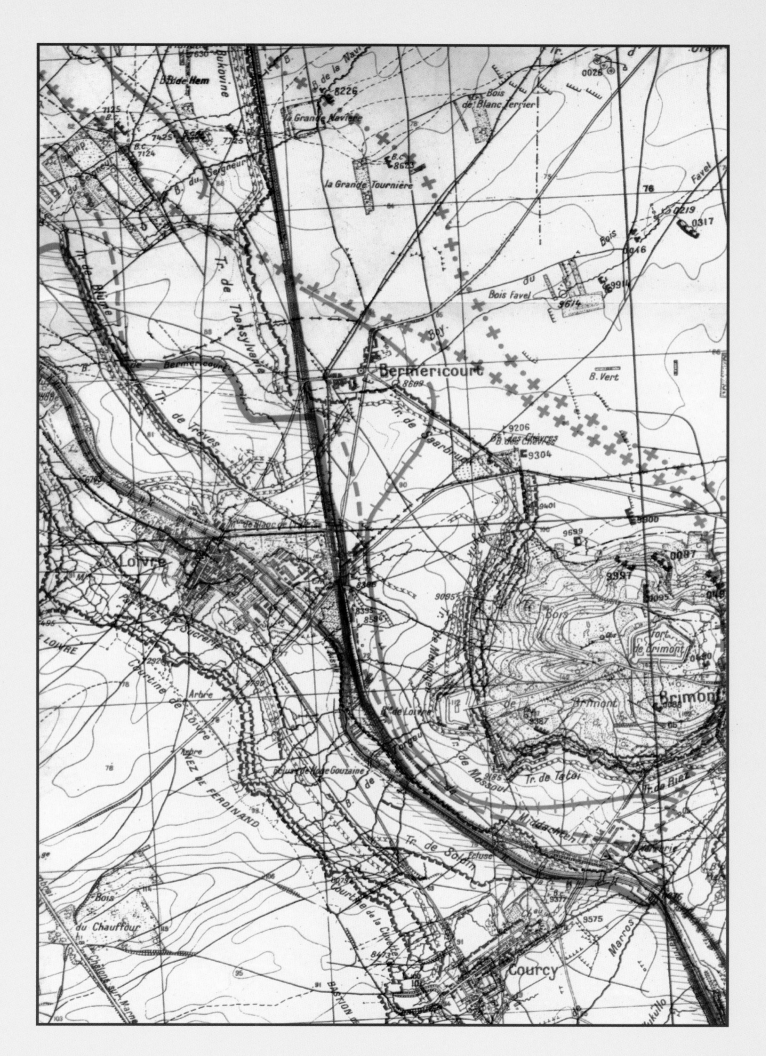

A Hotchkiss machine gun in an anti-aircraft position in the French redoubt of Anvers, in front of Loivre.

On the right of the front of attack, the 151ᵉ DI rushed at the road of Neuchâtel pocket and les Cavaliers de Courcy. Progress was rather fast and both objectives had been captured by 8 a.m. Beyond that, German machine guns once more were able to stop the assault. The enemy counter-attacked in the afternoon and the French could only keep the first line and backup line of the Neuchâtel pocket: the 403ᵉ RI repelled 19 counter-attacks!
(Archipel/BDIC)

At Châlons-sur-Vesle, close enough to fire at Brimont, a 400-mm gun is about to be loaded with a 915 kg shell.

To capture Brimont and the redoubt which overlooked the villages of Courcy and Loivre, the 7ᵉ corps launched forward the Russian brigade. Losses were very severe, but Courcy was taken around noon. The advance stopped at the edge of the canal and railway line, at the foot of the Brimont hill. On the left, the 41ᵉ division took the Luxembourg redoubt, then Loivre at about 2 p.m. It was ordered not to move further on.
(BDIC)

On the 5ᵉ armée right flank

In Loivre, the dug-outs of German gunners have been captured.

Right north of Loivre, the 14ᵉ DI achieved a superb advance, taking not just the first enemy line but the second too, and reaching the village of Berméricourt. But on its left the 37ᵉ DI was strongly pushed back in front of mont Spin and retreated, leaving the left flank of the 14ᵉ DI unprotected. The Germans realized this and launched a strong counter-attack after 3 p.m. In very difficult conditions the French were thrown back in two stages, but could still managed to hang on to the outskirts of Berméricourt.
(BDIC/Archipel)

Ambulance 4/1 at Châlons-sur-Vesle.

The 37ᵉ division was stopped in front of the first enemy trench line by the machine guns at mont Sapin. Their advance amounted to very little. After a fresh endeavour of the artillery against mont Sapin and mont Sapigneul, the infantry launched another assault around noon but was no more successful than in the morning. There were heavy losses as German counter-attacks drove the units' remnants back to their starting point. The 3ᵉ brigade russe was called in as reinforcement.
(BDIC/Archipel)

The 3ᵉ Tirailleurs going down from the front lines in front of Brimont, in April 1917.

The Brimont sector, just behind the redoubt, was home to several German batteries whose fire was felt not only on Courcy and Loivre, at the foothill, but also, in enfilade fire, on the surroundings of mont Spin and mont Sapigneul. The impossibility of capturing Brimont thus proved a great handicap.
(Archipel/BDIC)

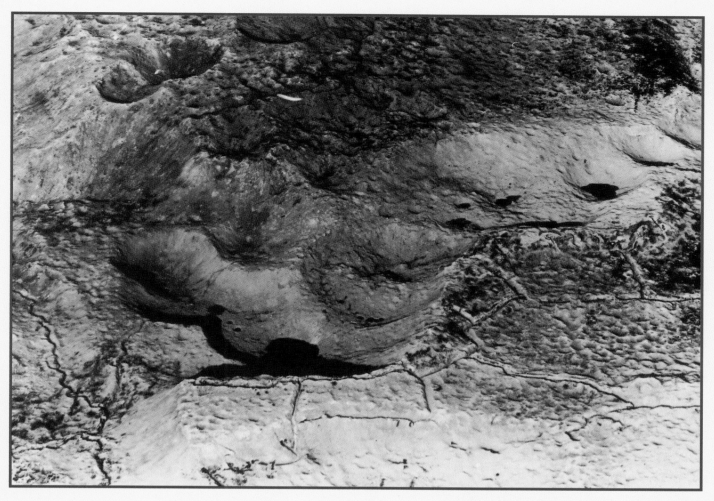

A picture of hell: hill 108 photographed from an altitude of 2,600 feet.

Controlling hill 108 was important to the 32ᵉ corps as this position overlooked Berry-au-Bac, from where Bossut's tanks were to leave for Juvincourt. North of the Aisne, two divisions attacked in more or less close cooperation with the tanks: the 42ᵉ and 69ᵉ.
The 42ᵉ DI quickly captured the first German line, then the first trenches of the second line. After that they waited for the tanks, which were behind schedule as will be seen in the next pages.
(BDIC/Archipel)

Waiting in a dug-out.

The 69ᵉ DI took the first two German lines, but the troops were pounded by heavy artillery and it became impossible to move on. Passaga, whose left wing had advanced farther than the right, was in a difficult situation at the foot of mont Sapigneul and asked for fresh troops. He even wished to bring the 40ᵉ DI back to their starting positions in order to launch a new, consistent assault. General Mazel strongly disagreed and answered: "*It is out of the question to give up the trenches conquered at mont Sapigneul*".
(BDIC/Archipel)

Bossut and his Schneider tanks

The Schneider tanks
en route for the Aisne. ▲

There is no better summary of the battle plan of French tanks than a note of 30 June 1917 written by major-general's aide de Barescut from the GQG. Here is the relevant quotation: "*16 April. Considering the use of tanks as difficult and useless on a terrain which has been deeply dug up by artillery, it had been decided that they would take part in the attack of the third and fourth enemy lines. Two groups have been activated (...). The second group (Bossut), with 80 vehicles, was to attack between the rivers Aisne and Miette. Coming in from its standby position, one kilometer west of Pontavert, it had to approach, following the artillery, in a single column (because of the one bridge on the Miette), deploy in the vicinity of the Mauchamp farm (second enemy position) and from there attack the third line on the Damary farm-Guignicourt front*".
(BDIC/Archipel)

A side view
of a Schneider tank.

Four squadrons of the Bossut group fought alongside the 69e division d'infanterie and the fifth with the 42e DI. the supporting infantry consisted of five companies of the 154e RI. The squadrons engaged were the 2e, 4e, 5e, 6e and 9e. Each squadron was made up of 16 tanks, typically operating in batteries of four.
(BDIC/Archipel) ▼

◀ Schneider tanks, in front of which the crews are posing, did not like obstacles. This is why they were to attack beyond the first lines only.

Major Bossut's brother left this story: *"The tank column was built up again and set forth, this time on the road as day was about to break, making any traffic but ours impossible. It was hardly dawn yet when we drove through Pontavert and on to the road to Guignicourt which, up to the crossing of the Miette, had us run parallel to the front for three kilometers, close to and in sight of the enemy. They found us out approximately halfway through. Numerous batteries opened fire at us; it is an extraordinary thing that we suffered so little up to the Miette. When we got there, I could see that my brother's fears were only too founded. The first tanks had to cross in a column under terrible fire, then proceed along the river for a few hundred yards of chaotic terrain before they could find a place where they could deploy for battle".*
(BDIC/Archipel)

▼

Information on the tanks'
intervention trickled in.
One report to the commander
of the 5ᵉ armée, dated 16 April
at 5 p.m., came from captain
Chanoine, C.O. of the 6ᵉ groupe
d'AS: *"I respectfully inform you
that the tank attack of 16 April
has passed the second German
line between the Miette and
the Mauchamps farm by a very
short distance only (...). Many
tanks of my squadron and the
squadron of captain Pardon,
operating between the Miette
and Mauchamps, have been
set on fire by shells.
Concerning squadrons 4, 5, 9,
I also saw many tanks burning.
Major Bossut is among the
dead. I have no news of
captain de Forsanz, who
was the commanding officer.
I have ordered that after an
attack by the 155ᵉ and 151ᵉ RI,
that I will back up, the
remaining tanks return to the
point which was our standby
position on the Pontavert-Cuiry
road, one kilometre west of
Pontavert, where I will await
your orders. Many of the tanks
which were not burnt have
broken down on the second
German position. I will take
away all that I can".*
(BDIC/Archipel)

The Bossut group in the storm

General Passaga noted: *"After this day,
a very difficult one for the tanks, I am
wondering whether I can count on them
tomorrow for an efficient intervention".*
(BDIC/Archipel)

On the eve of the attack,
the crew of "Fleur d'Ajonc"
was in high spirits. ▲

"*A few machines were stopped by
enemy fire; others, including mine,
got into critical positions in shell
holes and could only get out again
after many attempts. For a few
minutes, as I was second in the
column, I was terribly afraid of
blocking the other 79 tanks which
in that spot had no way of getting
through either on the left or right.
One of my steering mechanisms
was broken and all I could do was
to get out of the hole to clear the
way (...). I cried with rage at our
helplessness to repair the tank,
and it was difficult for me to
follow the stages of the battle;
I saw tanks catching fire all
over the plain and the first
wounded men walking past
my vehicle; some tanks were
several kilometres ahead
of me and pushing on*".
(BDIC/Archipel)

A Schneider tank
on manoeuvres.

**Some models, such as
this one, had received extra
armour plating.**
(BDIC/Archipel) ▶

A very rare photograph of tank "Malèche" and its mascot. ▲

The tanks at Juvincourt

After his tank got bogged down, Pierre Bossut set off to look for his brother's, which he eventually identified thanks to the iron mast of its pennant that was still standing at the rear:

"*I first saw the almost charred remains of sergeant-major Duyff who had been able to crawl about twenty yards away from his tank before dying. Under the very tank's door was my poor brother, largely spared by fire, with a quiet composure on his face; his skull showed a number of wounds. A piece of shrapnel that had entered his chest near the heart and come out below his shoulder blade had certainly killed him instantly. There is no doubt that the major, blown out of the burning tank by the explosion, would have tried to get away from the blaze had he still had a breath of life in him*".
(BDIC /Archipel)

A three-quarter view of a Schneider.

Although fitted with a prow, the Schneiders did not enter a trench as a ship would a wave. Many got bogged before being burnt down by the artillery. ▶
(BDIC / Archipel)

Captain de Blic, C.O.
of AS 7, and his crew posing
in front of their machine.

General de Boissoudy, C.O. of the 5ᵉ corps d'armée, described the intervention of the Chaubès group: *"During this advance the five sections of the 76ᵉ RI, whose task it was to clear the ground in front of the tanks, followed the assault troops and arrived at the enemy trenches at the same time as the mopping up wave. Work on the first German trench, 9 feet wide and very deep, was not complete when the first tank turned up. It nevertheless attempted to get through, tilted forward and obstructed the way which had begun to get cleared. Behind it the other tanks, under fierce shelling, stopped for a moment then attempted to deploy in order to look for another way through. During this move, several were set on fire or damaged by the enemy artillery and remained where they were; none could get through the first line".* (BDIC/Archipel)

Captain de Boisgelin, C.O.
of AS 7, posing in front
of a picture of Joan-of-Arc.

The failure of the Chaubès group tanks was beyond question: none of the machines had been able to pass the first German line. Material losses were particularly heavy: 32 tanks were destroyed out of 48. The proportion was even worse for those tanks that had actually taken part in the battle: 32 out of 40, or 80%. The 8 Schneiders that returned from combat were all more or less damaged, but still able to move around. Squadron 3 had lost all its tanks, squadron 7 had five and squadron 8 three. The crews had 9 killed, 4 missing and 38 wounded. (BDIC/Archipel)

Close-up of a crapouillot.

Thanks to the tanks' advance, the 9e division could reach the vicinity of Juvincourt and held on to the second line in spite of a number of enemy counter-attacks. The artillery could not support the most advanced units properly, and only the crapouillots units could penetrate - with difficulty - into enemy ground.
(BDIC/Archipel)

At Huns' wood

A map of the Juvincourt sector.

The terrain was rather favourable to the use of tanks and their advance was better than elsewhere.
(SHAT)

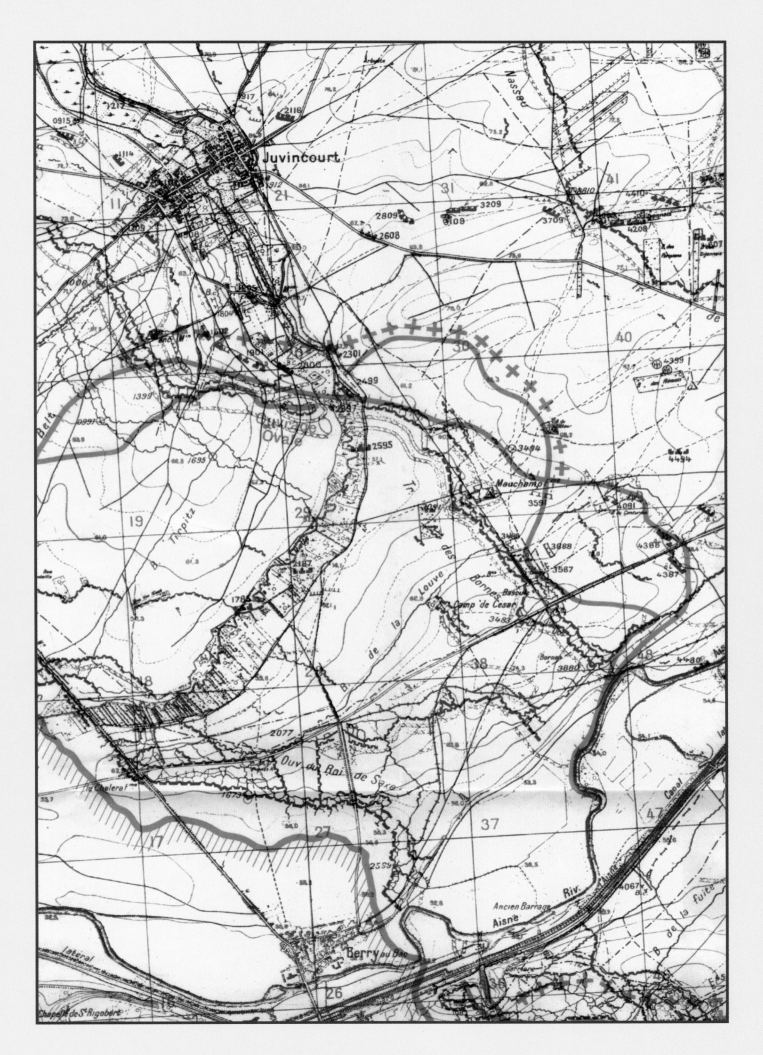

Craonne and the Californie plateau ▲

An aerial view
of Craonne and
the Californie plateau.

The photo was taken early in
June 1917. Six weeks before,
destructions were less visible.
Southeast of Craonne the
6e division advanced with
great difficulty towards Huns'
wood and Buttes wood.
It received no help from the
Chaubès group, as every of its
tanks had been stopped on
the first line. By the end
of the day, only Buttes wood
had been captured.
On the left, the 1er corps
attacked to the north. The
2e DI took Chevreux wood
and not much beyond that.
The most formidable task was
the 1re DI's whose first
objective was Craonne,
described in these words by
official history: "*a village
hanging on the bluff, below
the almost vertical wall of
the Californie plateau; the
enemy has observation posts
there with far-ranging views
of the French positions*".
Given the defense system
at Craonne, it would have
been surprising that the
division had been able to
advance, but it could
nevertheless climb the slopes
south of the village. On
the other hand, right around
Craonne and the plateau,
the losses were terrible and
the assault was stopped.

(BDIC)

A German photograph
of Craonne in 1916.

At 10.15 a.m. general
Muteau ordered a new
artillery preparation so
that the 1re and 2e divisions
could repeat their assault,
the former against Californie,
the latter towards Corbeny,
and the 162e against the
Vauclerc plateau. In spite
of the preparation, the
attacks were once again
stopped by machine guns,
particularly from Hurtebise
on the 6e armée's front,
which had not been captured
yet. At 2 p.m. a fresh assault
was launched. The 1re DI
made slight progress towards
Craonne, with losses that
were qualified as "cruel".
The 2e division was in a
truly dramatic situation,
under enfilade fire from
all sides and above all from
the heights of the
Californie plateau.
(BDIC/Archipel) ▶

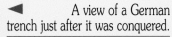 A view of a German trench just after it was conquered.

This lay between Craonne and Hurtebise, where the battle of 16 April was fiercest.. Here is general Muteau's account: *"The regiments set off exactly on time and were almost immediately submerged in the fire of the countless machine guns that concrete bunkers or natural caves had protected from our shelling; on the plain east of Craonne, a large number materialized right in the middle of the fields; the photographs (...) had not shown any evidence of them. This particular situation accounts for the high losses, the enemy artillery response not having been very fierce. (...). For the 2ᵉ DI the situation was critical. (...). A unit of chasseurs of the 66ᵉ DI had to go into the battle to stop a gap created by the almost total destruction of the 208ᵉ. This regiment has been reduced to a few remains".*
(BDIC)

French observers near Hurtebise.

Perfectly concealed from the French, nests of machine guns were disclosed at the very last moment.
(BDIC/Archipel)

German officers captured in front of Craonne.

On the front of the 5e armée the French captured about 7,000 prisoners, almost twice as many as the 6e armée. However the front was not ruptured and the day's gains, while more significant than for Mangin's army, were also more precarious: German counter attacks were to take back a large part of the terrain, to the high command's fury. (BDIC/Archipel)

An assessment of the day for the 5e armée

An ambulance at Beaurieux, at the foot of the Craonne and Hurtebise hills.

Losses were very heavy for the 1er corps: the 1re DI lost 1,257 men, the 2e 3,766 (including 1,641 for the 208e RI alone) and the 162e 1,538. A new attempt was almost impossible and it was difficult to hold the conquered ground. (BDIC/Archipel)

The conquered trenches were in complete upheaval.

The 1er corps had suffered such losses that its C.O. requested that the 2^e DI be relieved immediately. Here is the end of his report: *"Moreover it is my opinion that, given the fierceness of the fight on the Vauclerc plateau, we will have to replace the other infantry divisions by fresh units without delay if we want to push on or even hold the top of the plateaus".* The 37e and 40e DI of 5e armée had also suffered and the reserves only amounted to two divisions. For the next day the push would have to be directed at mont Spin in order to protect the flank of 144e DI in front of Brimont. But the main thrust would be where the tanks had gone farthest, thanks to the intervention of the 9e corps of 10e armée. Nivelle hoped he could still change the course of events. *(BDIC/Archipel)*

A map of the Craonne sector and the Californie plateau.

(SHAT

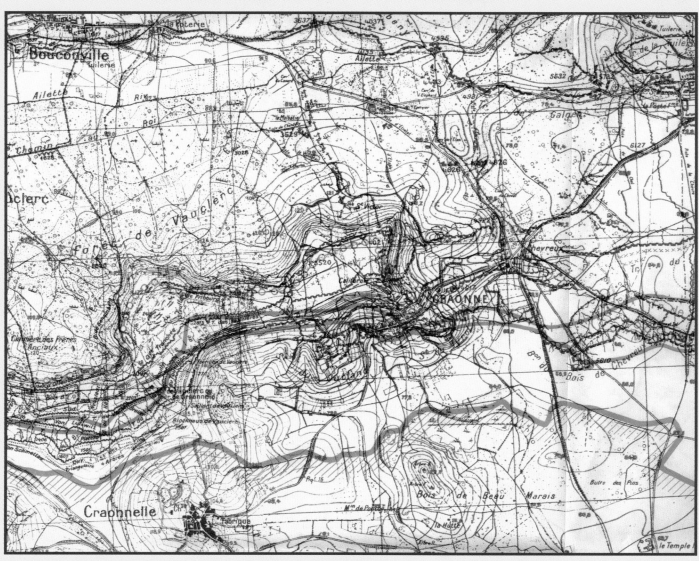

The battle
in the following days

THE failed 16 April attack did not mean the end of the battle, as Nivelle could not bring himself to stop his offensive. The first stage went on until 26 April, and the fighting continued into the first weeks of May. On 15 May, general Pétain was put at the head of the armées du Nord et du Nord-Est in Nivelle's place. He would bring an end to the fruitless fighting and begin to put the French army back on its feet, to eventually lead it to victory in 1918. April 17 was an important day as the 4ᵉ armée, east of Rheims, was joining in the attack. It may thus be argued that general Nivelle still had reason to hope and reverse a compromised situation. It will also be remembered that he had asked president Poincaré and minister Painlevé for 48 hours in order to break through the front. From the reports that had kept arriving in Compiègne at the GQG, Nivelle realized that he must give up all hope on the front of Mangin's army. Micheler, at the head of GAR, instructed Mangin to restrict the 6ᵉ armée to the partial conquest of Chemin des Dames. There was no mention of breaking the front now, as the troops' condition did not permit it and Micheler refused to engage even a single division from the 10ᵉ armée on the 6ᵉ's front.

In the night of 16 to 17 April rain kept pouring down. The 6ᵉ armée held to its positions except to the west where it abandoned Mont des Singes. In the morning Nivelle confirmed Micheler's orders: the Mangin army was to complete the capture of the southern reaches of the river Ailette and cover the chief offensive led by the 5ᵉ armée. The breakthrough phase was thus terminated and consequently the 5ᵉ division de cavalerie left the front. Fighting continued on a smaller scale than the day before and progress was meager, with a trench taken here and there. The only success of some scope was the capture of the Grinons ridge and the quarries south of Cour-Soupir, which permitted to outflank the plateau overlooking the Aisne at Soupir and Chavonne. On the front of the 5ᵉ armée, renewing the attack was useless, with poor weather preventing any artillery preparation. Combat was thus limited to a number of grenade attacks to strengthen precariously held positions, a full enumeration of which would be tedious. Only the 1ᵉʳ corps fought a hard battle trying to get a foothold on the Californie plateau. The day's fights were remarkably summed up by battalion C.O. Nicolas, whose comments can indeed apply to all of the other units engaged on that day: "*It is my feeling that despite the 1ᵉʳ Corps d'Armée's support, the situation cannot change on the Chevreux-Hurtebise front to the point of enabling us within a short time to advance towards the Ailette. We are down to communication trench fights, to equally impossible choices; such convulsions cannot lead to anything decisive. Will the 1ᵉʳ CA eventually be able on their own to take the Californie and the wood, that is to say occupy the entire plateau? Quite sincerely, I doubt it, and all the present artillery fire will not change that*".

While the front of attack of 16 April remained largely unchanged, the 4ᵉ armée launched its offensive in the Champagne region. Without getting into a detailed account, it is worth noting that the advance ranged from 500 metres to 2.5 kilometers, which was more than on the Aisne. Several German observation positions were captured, including mont Sans-Nom and mont Blond. The battle went on until 20 April, but as no breakthrough could be expected general Pétain, who was heading the groupe d'armées du Centre, tried instead to keep the first day's gains and expand them systematically. The southern trenches of mont Cornillet were taken, as were most of mont Blond, mont Haut, le Casque and mont Sans-Nom as well as the Golfe and the village of Aubérive-sur-Suippe. 3,550 German soldiers and 27 guns were captured.

► The ruins of Soupir seen from the captured German positions.

On 17 April, the 127ᵉ DI strengthened its position in the sector and repelled all German counter-attacks against Mont Sapin. A Senegalese battalion of 56ᵉ DI took the Grinons ridge.
(BDIC)

▲

In a first line
dug-out at Hurtebise.

A chaplain is sitting on the right with a beard and a stick.
(Archipel/BDIC)

An unexpected German retreat

The quarries of Cour-Soupir converted into a field hospital. ►

On 18 April, after a new attack was launched by the 6e armée, a German retreat movement began, then gained momentum. It had no doubt been planned since the day before and aimed at evacuating the whole area of the Condé salient. This had become too insecure since the French had managed to cling to part of the Chemin des Dames ridge. The Germans had moreover suffered substantial losses in the last three days and the move allowed them to shorten their front. La Cour-Soupir was captured by the 127e DI. The German retreat was quick. *(Archipel/BDIC)*

▲ Lieutenant Pochard,
on the right, and his N.C.O.s.

Lieutenant Pochard was the C.O. of 2e compagnie / 1er bataillon / 132e RI. He is seen here
with his N.C.O.s, from left to right: warrant
officer Dey, sergeant Ravier, sergeant Baron
and sergeant Debarge. The picture was taken
on 28 May 1917 at Chemin des Dames after
they were awarded a croix de guerre, probably
for taking the village of Braye on 17 April.
This is how lieutenant Pochard described the
action: *"5.30 p.m. The company sets off.
They have never manoeuvred so well, it is
superb. I weep with joy. Snow is falling, but
never mind; so much the better for us on the
contrary... The tack-tack begins. We can no
longer advance in the open, only from one
shell hole to another. Dead men of the
7e compagnie in the Unstrutt trench - so
they came as far as here yesterday morning.
The huns are shelling us. Each man proges-
sing on his own. 3 or 4 machine guns are
firing at us, one kilometre away. I can see a
few on the slopes, east of Braye. Our
machine guns respond. On our right we can
see men of the 20e corps advancing.
Sunshine again. We have reached our
objective. Patrolling along the canal
towards Braye. It is 7.45 p.m. Here are
some huns coming up with hands raised;
carrying bundles and shoes on their backs.
51 of them. They make off quicly"*.
(Pochard photo, F. Vauvillier Collection)

Mess call in one of
the "creutes" of Chemin des Dames.

The caves, creutes and stone quarries were a
basic feature in the battle of Chemin des Dames.
It is surprising that the high command should
have ignored this when selecting a terrain for the
offensive for, as was discussed previously, while
the artillery had destroyed a fair number of
German batteries but it could not destroy these
natural bunkers. The Germans used them for
their own protection and the protection of
their machine guns during the artillery
preparation. (Archipel/BDIC) ◄

The Mangin army gains ground

Two views of the top of Mont Sapin: a German graveyard and a conquered trench.

The Germans abandoned a large area on 18 April: they left the Aisne valley, which was no longer of any use to them, moving back to Chemin des Dames. Before leaving the villages they burnt them down: Vailly, Aisy, Sancy, Jouy, the Rochefort farm. Occasionally the retreat was interrupted by fierce counter-attacks, as at Mont Sapin in the morning of 18 April. German prisoners taken nearby, at the Grinons, said they had been ordered to fall back on the Siegfried Stellung, i.e. on the ridge of Chemin des Dames. The news that part of the battle ground had been evacuated brought some relief at the GQG: *"Hope came back on the evening of 18 April. The Mangin army was looking at an enemy who was shunning them; the Mitry corps sent a series of telegrams telling of the capture of guns and large quantities of equipment. We had taken Ostel, Braye-en-Laonnais, Nanteuil-la-Fosse and our troops were moving on,"* Jean de Pierrefeu wrote.
(Archipel/BDIC)

A map of the evacuated sector.

(SHAT)

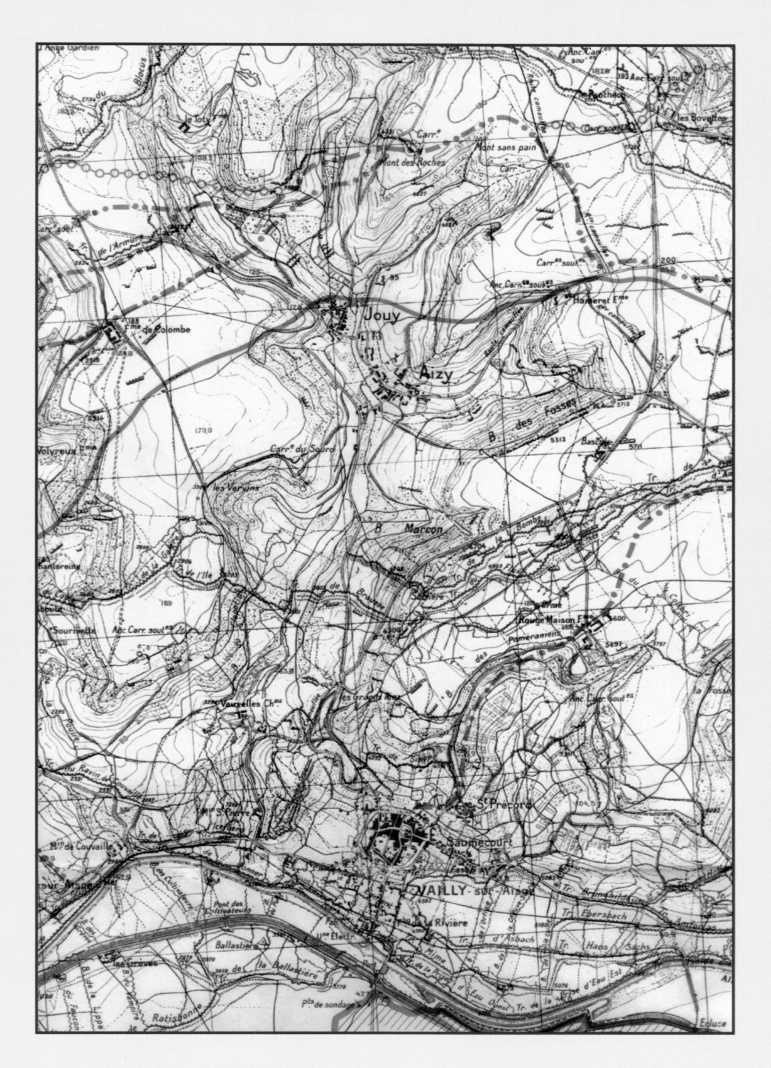

German prisoners on
a road near Bazoches-sur-Vesle.

On 19 April the 5ᵉ armée made
about 500 prisoners, bringing
the total since 16 April to 4,500.
Apart from this, the situation
had not changed much on the
front. The Hurtebise monument
was taken, as well as the Cerny
sugarmill, but this was
taken back by the Germans.
The exhausted 2ᵉ corps
was relieved by the 11ᵉ.
(Archipel/BDIC)

A shelter for
the wounded near Soupir.

German prisoners were used
to carry the wounded. There
was no animosity between the
two sides, except in letters
home: relatives would not
have understood otherwise.
(BDIC/Archipel)

The battle bogs down

A mess detail is about
to go down into a creute.

Mess and ammo duty and
relieving units were not easy
because of bad weather and
the German shelling. The broken
up ground was very muddy.
Front line units were getting
more and more tired and were
in no position to interfere
with the German retreat and
outmanoeuvre them, which
Nivelle regretted on a number
of occasions. In any case
ammunition stocks were
getting depleted and Micheler
had instructed to use
them sparingly.
(BDIC/Archipel)

The difficult ride
of a 155 Schneider up
a muddy slope.

On 19 April, the 6e corps
was ordered to take a group
of artillery up to Cour-Soupir.
It was a dreadful task and up
to 18 horses per vehicle were
needed to handle it!
(Archipel/BDIC)

Progress of the 6ᵉ armée between 17 and 20 April

▲ A 75-mm gun has exploded from over-intensive use.

The infantry suffered greatly during the Chemin des Dames offensive, though not because of insufficient artillery support. On 20 April the battle was quieter. General Mangin sent a report to the GQG insisting on gains, but Nivelle knew better: the German retreat had been orderly and French troops had never been able to outmanoeuvre the enemy. However public opinion knew nothing of this and Mangin's self-propaganda was fairly clever: *"Over 12 kilometres along the Aisne, from Soupir to Missy-sur-Aisne, our line south of the river has advanced by 6 to 7 kilometres. The Condé redoubt (...), the villages of Chivy, Bray-en-Laonnais, Ostel, Chavonne, Vailly, Celles, Condé-sur-Aisne, Laffaux, Nanteuil-la-Fosse, Sancy, Jouy, Aisy, have fallen into our hands (...). The observation posts that the enemy had over the Aisne valley are now ours, along with others at Chemin-des-Dames, giving us views over the Ailette valley and beyond"*.
(BDIC)

A captured 77-mm gun.

Mangin went on to note that 80 guns had been captured.
(BDIC)

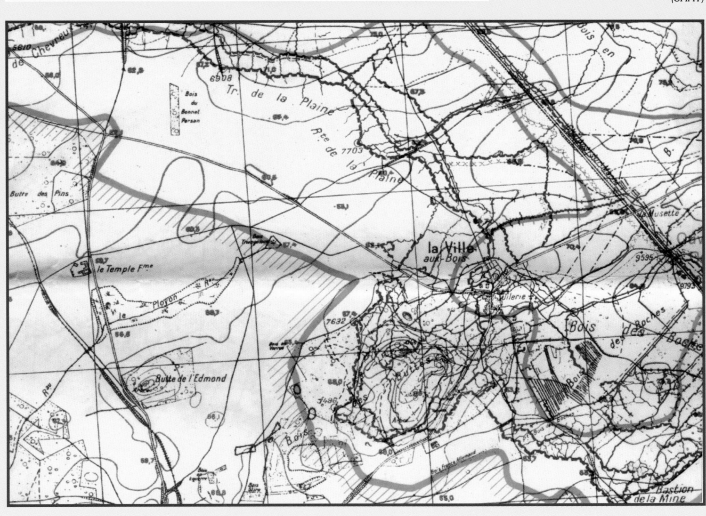

A Hotchkiss machine gun in action near Craonne.

Weather was too bad on 18 April on the 5e armée's front for the planned attacks to be launched, except against Huns' wood and Ville-aux-Bois which were captured and yielded plentiful bounty: 1,300 prisoners and a number of guns. While the front was pushed forward as far as one mile away from Juvincourt, breaking it was now out of the question. The greatest success of the day was defensive. Here is how *Les Armées Françaises dans la Grande Guerre* described it: *"Today's event was a failed attack by two German divisions at least, starting at about 4 p.m. between the Aisne and Juvincourt. Our heavy and field artilleries responded quickly and caused serious losses in the enemy's ranks. Their disrupted units were kept away from our trenches by rifle and machine-gun fire. A second attempt failed completely"*.
On 19 April the French resumed their offensive and failed both in Bermericourt and monts Sapin and Sapigneul: *"Machine-guns which had not been shelled out caused the attack to fail"*.
At Craonne, the 1er corps made a new attempt against Californie, which was taken, then lost again. In the village itself, progress was hard and undecisive. The next day was quieter. Stage one of the battle of the Aisne was coming to a close.
(Archipel/BDIC)

Map of the Ville-aux-Bois sector.

(SHAT)

The 5ᵉ armée front

German prisoners
taken at Craonne.

Between 16 and 20 April,
the 5ᵉ armée captured
11,000 prisoners, 40 guns
and 200 machine-guns.
(BDIC/Archipel)

A general view
of Chemin des Dames.

Only the first enemy
line had been taken.
(BDIC)

The offensive continues

ALTHOUGH the anticipated breakthrough had failed, and contrary to what he had said before the attack, general Nivelle was determined to push on with operations between Soissons and Rheims. Indeed he wrote to general Haig: "*Although the advance of our attacking armies is slower than expected, I change nothing to the general instructions for the offensive that I gave previously*".

However criticisms began to be voiced, not only in the parlement and government, but also within the army itself. Thus on 21 April general Micheler listed a number of reasons why the offensive shouldn't be carried on. His four arguments were: 1) The Germans had fallen back on the Siegfried line. 2) The attacks against Craonne on the one hand, mont Sapigneul on the other, had failed: consequently the flanks of a northeast attack would be exposed. 3) Fresh units were reduced to four divisions. 4) Ammunition stocks were insufficient for a new offensive. As a conclusion he wrote: "*... the question is raised whether or not to carry out the plan completely (...). The proposed exploitation north of the Aisne cannot be contemplated without a new general offensive over the whole front, given the need to cover the flanks. GAR does not have the means for this, which will no doubt demand supplementary forces, either to feed the attack or for reliefs. One may furthermore wonder whether, in the present circumstances, the front of attack of GAR can possibly be exploited against a well-warned enemy who has had time to rally. Past experience should advise us against delusions in this respect.*"

Since the fight must continue, Micheler suggested actions of limited scope aiming at building up positions on Chemin des Dames, monts Sapin and Sapigneul, and Brimont.

Clearly neither Nivelle, his superior, nor Mangin, his subordinate, liked the idea. The latter even wrote to his wife on that very day:

Going up to the front through the village of Craonne, in French lines. ▲

Craonne and the Californie plateau are a short distance to the north.
(Author's collection)

Map of ►
May 1917 offensive
(SHAT))

"*I think I will soon be rid of Micheler.*" Indeed incompatibility was such between Micheler and Mangin that on 26 April Nivelle decided to transfer the 6e armée from GAR to Franchet d'Espéray's groupe d'armées du Nord.

Le paragraphe manquant commence ici...

Le paragraphe manquant fini ici... et suite et fin du texte.

At the sanded attributions, was given to general Pétain. He was to advise the government and keep an eye on Nivelle.

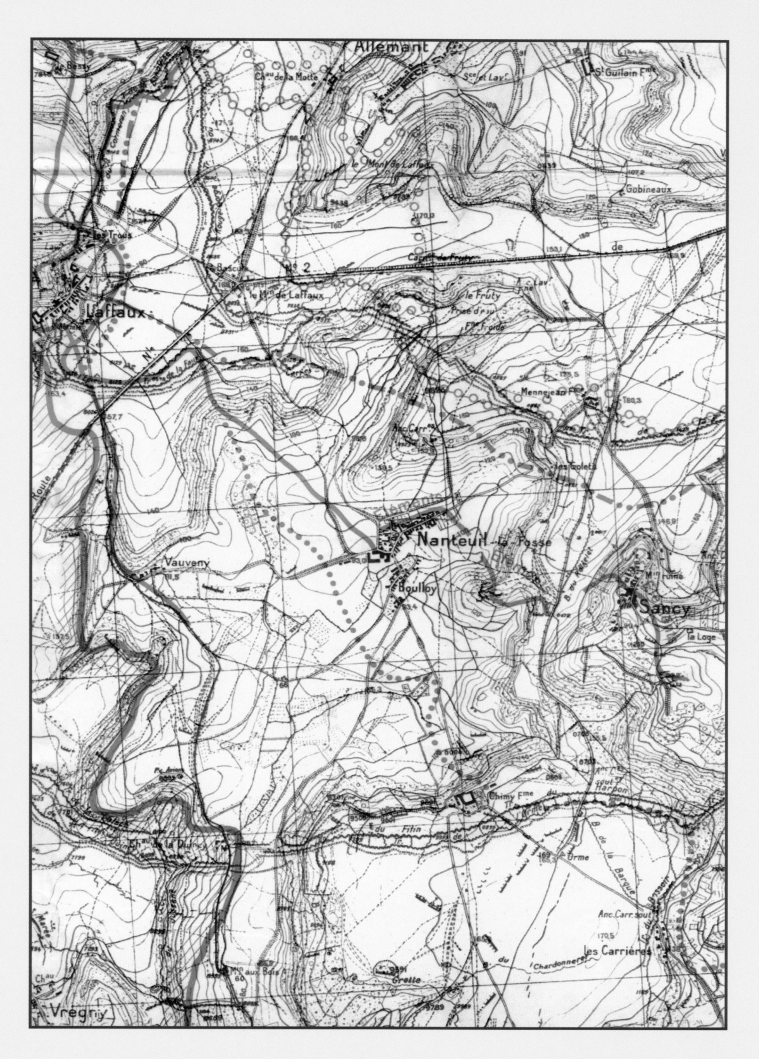

Pétain, a providential man

▲ General Pétain embracing aviation captain d'Harcourt.

The appointment of Pétain as general chief-of-staff came as a clear warning to Nivelle. He thought he could save himself by sacrificing Mangin, to whom he sent this message on 30 April: *"My dear Mangin, I am forced to take note of the fact that you no longer have your subordinates' trust and, in agreement with the war minister and to my deep regret, have no choice but to put you on the inactive list. It is a sad and painful duty for me to have to cause a faithful* comrade-in-arms so much sorrow (...)."* Mangin was relieved of his command and even barred from visiting Paris and the surrounding départements! He was perfectly clear-minded about this. *"I think general Nivelle thought he could make concessions by throwing me overboard".* This however was not to be enough. General Nivelle's fate had already been decided by the government. One man only seemed able to remain cold-headed in the painful circumstances: the man who had saved Verdun one year before, Philippe Pétain. His time came on 15 May 1917. *(Archipel/BDIC)*

Generals Pétain and Nivelle.

This double colour photograph gives a fairly good image of the two men's personalities. Pétain, on the left, is wearing a plain uniform. He has no desire to show off and his pre-war career has not been an opportunist's. His theories were always disliked at the Ecole de Guerre. In 1914 he was about to retire as a colonel. His clear-sightedness in the first months of the war boosted his career. A specialist of well-prepared attacks - or, rather, as well-prepared as possible, given the constant lack of means - he owed his national fame to his remarkable achievement in the defense of Verdun between February and May 1916. Verdun was a springboard for general Robert Nivelle too. The successor of Pétain at the head of the 2ᵉ armée, he led mostly unsuccessful attacks to recapture lost ground in May onwards, then obtained significant results in October and December 1916.

An obscure colonel in 1914, just like Pétain, he had an even more dazzling career since in December 1916 he replaced Joffre at the head of French armies. With extreme self-confidence, he was sure he could break the German front in 48 hours, where he chose to, and was able to convince the government. The failure of 16 April left him in a difficult position: he had promised too much. Summoned at the Elysée palace on 25 April, he did not depart from his self-confidence, claiming he had won "*the most brilliant of all strategic victories (...). We have the initiative of operations and will keep it, as I will show*". President Poincaré did not buy this, nor did minister Painlevé. The appointment of Pétain as general chief-of-staff is ample evidence. But the two men left Nivelle a chance. Developments in the early May attacks, which will be discussed in the next pages, hastened his downfall. Jean de Pierrefeu, a privileged observer at the GQG,

gave this account: "*General Nivelle's departure was uncere-monious. Rarely had a top-ranking general vanished from the scene in such indifference. While he was still in command, he had ceased to exist in every-body's eyes. The real chief was awaited every day with hardly concealed impatience. On the day when it was announced he was coming to Compiègne, a quiver of joy ran through the whole place, except maybe the 3ᵉ bureau. There was something supernatural in the man' aura*". Nivelle's downfall came in three stages: Pétain's appoint-ment as general chief-of-staff in April, then a personal letter from Painlevé on 15 May: "*I have the honour to inform you that the government of the Republic has decided, as of May 15 1917, to appoint major general Pétain at the head of the armées du Nord et du Nord-Est. The decree dated December 12 1916 by which you were given this command is therefore revoked.*

As a consequence you will please return the warrant of command which is now in your possession". On the same day Poincaré officially notified Nivelle that he was to command a group of armies on the North and Northeast front. But the comfort was short-lived. Pétain, the new generalissimo, sent him this message on 28 June: "*... I have at the moment no particular mission to entrust you with. Nor can I foresee any vacancy in a group of armies command in the near future. In the circumstances I therefore have to put you temporarily on the inactive list, until new developments in the war allow me to call on your collaboration and devoted service*". Put on rest leave, Nivelle was eventually appointed commander-in-chief of the troops in North Africa in December 1917, which kept him away for good from the important front.
(Author's Collection)

▼

A panoramic view
of the front, with the French
Finger lines on the left and the
German Tit lines on the right.

The photo was taken in the
Hurtebise sector, where the
10ᵉ armée entered the battle
on 4 May 1917. This was only
a preliminary attack, but an
important one nevertheless as
the objective was the village of
Craonne. The 18ᵉ RI soon took it,
at the cost of only 100 men killed
or wounded. The southern edge
of the Californie plateau was
taken too, but in order to reach
the ridge of Chemin des Dames
there remained to get a foothold
in the forest of Vauclerc.
(BDIC/Archipel)

The 10ᵉ armée is entering the fight

The entrance
to the Dragon's cave.

Colonel Havard, in charge
of the Hurtebise sub-sector, is
examining a German voltmetre
found in the cave.
(BDIC)

A party of gunners wearing gas masks.

On 4 May 1917, the 5e armée attacked as well towards monts Spin and Sapigneul, which Nivelle was bent on taking. The artillery preparation had begun on 29 April, but the Germans repaired the wire during the night. Also, they drowned the French with gas shells. A very violent shelling on Rheims destroyed the city hall and started several fires. The 41e division rushed at Berméricourt and entered the village, but the enemy counter-attacked and by 1 p.m. *"all communications were impossible with the heroic defenders of the village, surrounded and heavily shelled by German artillery"*. At the end of the day the division was thrown back to its starting line with significant losses. In front of monts Spin and Sapigneul it was a similar failure: the enemy shelters *"have suffered but little from shells although the ground is broken up; countless machine guns have appeared, sometimes even in our men's backs, on very tricky terrain"*.
(Imperial War Museum)

▲ A German defender at Chemin des Dames.

The Prussian Garde was engaged in the defense of the Californie plateau, which the Germans did not want to lose. It suffered very heavily in front of the Basques and Béarnais.
(Bundesarchiv)

▼

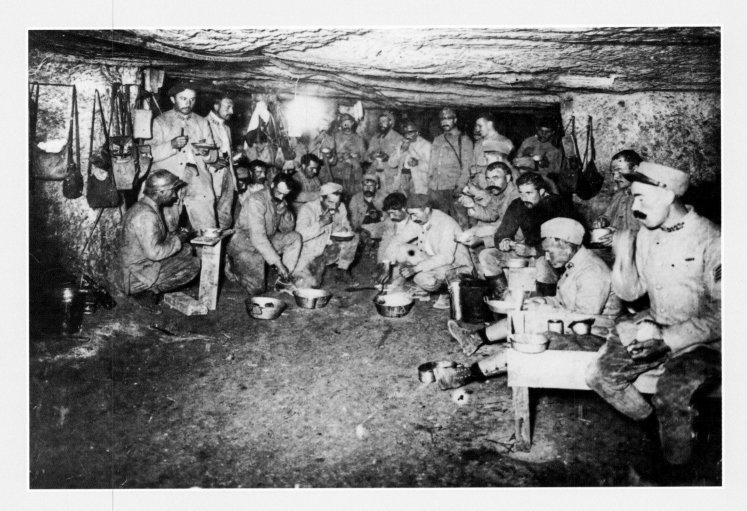

Mess call in the Elephant's cave and French graves in the Dragon's cave.

Hell at Craonne and Hurtebise

At 9 a.m. on 5 May, the 18ᵉ corps of the 10ᵉ armée launched its main assault against Craonne and Hurtebise farm, with two divisions (35ᵉ and 36ᵉ) abreast. In spite of the fierce resistance of the Garde corps, the Californie plateau was taken, but the French troops engaged on the Vauclerc plateau were attacked from behind by strong German contingents pouring out of the Dragon's and Saxons' caves. Testimonies quoted by Nobécourt are revealing: *"We advanced in the morning, but when we got through, the huns were coming out of holes and shooting us in the back. Many were killed or wounded".* *"The 65ᵉ attacked yesterday morning. At first it went very well. But (...) we went past our objectives and found ourselves caught between fires: huns in front and huns behind. We incurred heavy losses and we have no officers left. In the company there were 180 of us; hardly 40 are left today".* **Another soldier wrote to his wife:** *"What a day, my Mimi! All our objectives had been reached at noon; this morning they were all lost again".*
(BDIC)

180

◀ The kitchens
of a field dressing
station at Beaurieux.

The French failure on the
Vauclerc plateau and in front of
monts Spin and Sapigneul
caused fresh losses which were
paintless and ruined both French
morale and Nivelle's chances of
remaining at the head of French
armies. It seemed that a new
battle of the Somme was about
to be repeated, whereas
the generalissimo had loudly
proclaimed that he would not
do the same mistake as Joffre.
Moreover the losses had no
compensation, as the few
"*liberated*" villages had been
captured thanks to the
German retreat.
(BDIC/Archipel)

Camouflaged vehicles
in the village of Sermoise.

Never had such means been
used for such mediocre results
since the front was stabilized, and
never had disappointment been
so profound, matching equally
strong hopes. The fights of May
1917 were fought without
the slightest hope. ▼
(BDIC/Archipel)

◀ Wounded men
being evacuated at Beaurieux.

Losses kept going up on the
three armies' fronts. In a macabre
breakdown requested by the
Brugère board inquiry after the
battle, Nivelle calculated
the average losses per division in
the different offensives:
In Champagne in 1915, they were
2,500; On the Somme in 1916,
between 2,000 and 2,350; finally at
Chemin des Dames 2,600. As the
strengths in divisions were going
down (from 17,500 in 1915 to
13 or 14,000 in 1917), the rate
was getting higher. No really exact
count can be found on the number
of losses between 16 April and
10 May, but the 1er bureau gave
this total in January 1920:
3,727 officers and 135,862 men.
(BDIC)

A terrible
and desperate fight

In the cellars of the Hurtebise farm.

The battle of May 1917 was a horrible one and cold numbers speak
for themselves: the 11e corps, between the small spur at Hurtebise
and the Cerny sugarmill, lost 1,650 men in 24 hours. Nobécourt left
this description of an attack by the 102e bataillon de chasseurs à pied
against the trenches of Fiume and the Pirate: "*They almost
immediately came up against uncrossable wire networks.
They were standing abreast, unprotected from the waist up, while
the Germans were throwing grenades at them "with extraordinary
gusto" and machine guns - one every ten metres - kept them under
continuous fire. The first wave was almost entirely mowed down
and the second whirled around: a hundred chasseurs were
gone. The 102e BCP was relieved on that very evening*".
The French soldiers' letters all express the same feeling of horror:
"*The communiqué did say that we had repossessed most of the
ridge along Chemin des Dames, but it forgot to mention that one
hour later we had to scamper away with the huns at our backs;
they came out like ants*". Or this one: "*It was hell! I don't know how
I got out of it. Out of 700 in the battalion, there are only 260 left*".
Progress was limited to the capture of a few hundred metres of
trenches which were lost again more often than not. German counter-
attacks made it impossible to hold to the northern slope of
the Vauclerc plateau.
(BDIC/Archipel)

▶

Another view of
the scene on page 182.

Official records give a slightly
lower number of 134,000 men,
but it applies to the period of 16
to 25 April only. The breakdown is:
30,000 killed;
100,000 wounded;
4,000 prisoners
It is impossible to extrapolate with
any certainty on the very costly
attacks of May. But the cumulated
numbers of killed and missing men
between 16 April and 10 May are
over 50,000 according to the
1er bureau's study - which on the
other hand minimized the number
of wounded. By crosschecking
numbers, the following estimate
can be given:
dead: 48,000;
wounded 120,000;
prisoners 4,500.
The total is 172,500, including
20,000 with light wounds.
(BDIC/Archipel)

A German soldier killed in the fights at the Laffaux mill.

At the Laffaux mill

The first signs of a serious morale crisis appeared in the Laffaux sector on 4 May: one company refused to fight. In some quarters tracts were found with the words: "*Down with the war! Death to those in charge!*". In his thesis on the 1917 mutinies, Guy Pédroncini observes that most cases of rebellion were found in the 6e armée (formerly Mangin's) and among the divisions engaged in the May 1917 operations, which, as was shown, were the most useless. The attack at the Laffaux mill, although supported by Schneider and Saint-Chamond tanks, was no exception. In the 1er corps colonial, losses were again terrible for insignificant results. A poilu wrote: "*It was just as well if we all died, as those who didn't this time would the next. If we all have to go through it, better now than later*". The cuirassiers à pied still managed to take the Laffaux mill and to hold it against counter-attacks.
(BDIC/Archipel)

A destroyed German gun at Allemant.

An objective on 16 April, then on 5 May, Allemant was eventually only captured in October 1917 during the attack prepared by Pétain. *(BDIC)*

 Schneider tanks
going into battle.

The Lefebvre group fought in the battle of 5-6 May, with Schneider tanks in the AS 1 and 10 and Saint-Chamond tanks - appearing on the front for the first time - in AS 31. Their use was definitely more successful than on 16 April: in particular, none was destroyed by the enemy. Clearly, the tanks were of great help to the infantry advancing towards the Laffaux mill. But after four or five hours of fighting, the crews were exhausted.
(Author's Collection)

A CVII Albatros escaped
French fire above Rheims
and returned to its base.

According to a number of testimonies, German aircraft often attacked the infantry on the battlefield. *(BA)*

An AEG CIV after an emergency landing.

170 aircraft of this type were in use on the western front in April-May 1917. They were used for all kinds of observation and artillery cooperation missions. Its maximum speed was about 62 mph. It was armed with a Spandau machine gun at the front and a Parabellum for the observer. Towards the end of spring 1917, the German technical superiority lost its edge as numerous new allied fighters came into service: the British SE 5a, then the Sopwith Camel, and the French Spad VII.
(BDIC/Archipel)

A Saint-Etienne machine gun in anti-aircraft position.

The scene is in the Aisne valley in May 1917. After the failure of the attacks in the first two weeks of May, the battle was coming to a close.
(Author's Collection)

Air warfare above the Aisne

A 1905 model anti-aircraft searchlight and its tractor. ▲

In the year 1917 the first lessons of 1916 - when a theory of the use of aircraft came into being - were applied both by the Germans and Allies.
(BDIC/Archipel)

Georges Guynemer's Spad VII.

Guynemer came to the Bonnemaison airfield to join the offensive of Chemin des Dames. He won his 36th victory on 14 April at la Neuville. The month of May was a lucky one for him, with a kill at Courtemont on the 2nd, another above Braye on the 4th and, chiefly, four victories on the 25th: a two-seater shot down above Corbeny at 8.30 a.m., another one at Juvincourt one minute later, then a DFW at Courlandon at 12.15 p.m., and finally one more two-seater at 6.30 p.m. between Guignicourt and Condé-sur-suippes. Two days later he was to win his 43rd kill at Auberive. In May 1917, Fonck, then a rookie, shot down four planes in the Chemin des Dames sector. Nungesser was not in that sector. Georges Mado, the fourth French ace, also shot down four planes above the Aisne.
(Author's Collection) ▶

Lost illusions and morale crisis

Reserve French and British troops at le Verquier during the German fallback to the Hindenburg line.

Started almost triumphantly with the German retreat, the year 1917 turned out to be one of disillusionment. True, the United States had entered the war with the Allies in early April, but they had no army. On the British side, the remarkable achievement of 9 april 1917 could not be used to really break through the German front, and the first victories could not conceal the fact that the battle of Arras had been one of the most deadly ever fought by the British army. The last British illusions were to vanish in the mud of Passchendaele, in front of Ipres, while the near-success of Cambrai in November would be cancelled by a lightning counter-attack by Ludendorff, foreshadowing the great offensives of 1918. On the French side disillusionment was even worse, so much hope had the army and country placed in the new commander-in-chief, general Nivelle. The complete failure of the assaults of 16 April and 5 May shattered the very foundations of the army. In order to save it, the government called on the man of lost causes. Ducasse, Meyer and Perreux have expressed better than anyone else what Pétain's arrival at the head of the army represented: "*It is not an overstatement to say that, even more than after the Marne in 1914, the June 1917 recovery was the greatest miracle of the time, a miracle of psychology. The soldiers were so grateful for being at last understood by a man who spared their blood, that this explains the admiration and faithfulness they bore for their general when, twenty-three years later, he became head-of-state. That politics and warfare are not one and the same thing, that an eighty-year-old man no longer was what he had been at sixty, these make no doubt. But surely it is necessary to insist on the reasons for such long popularity - something that the younger generation cannot understand*".
André Bridoux, of the 2e Zouaves, told of the impression left after a visit by Pétain: "*Everyone was moved, for they had seen a rare thing: a leader who was also a man, and who seemed to be up to his task and the times*". As the Army's physician, Pétain improved his men's daily life, stepped up the schedule of leaves, and even accelerated leave trains, which had absolute priority over all other trains. In order to stop the mutinies, he ordered a limited number of executions (45 only for cases of insubordination) and called on almost all divisions. Another key element in Pétain's success in 1917 was his conception of warfare. For the first time he was completely free to put his theories into practise. In October 1917 on the Ailette and at la Malmaison, he had a remarkable tactical success on the very terrain of the April failure. Total French losses only reached 14,000, of whom a low proportion were killed, while 12,000 German prisoners were captured. No fewer than two million 75-mm shots were fired, along with 850,000 heavy artillery shells. For the first time, the poilus did not feel they were cannon fodder. It may be objected that the war could not have been won with battles such as la Malmaison. But Pétain had patience: he was waiting for the tanks and the Americans. The former would in fact be too late for this campaign, but not the tanks.
(IWM)

▶

TABLE OF CONTENTS

CHAPTER 1
From Joffre's plan to the German withdrawal of March 1917
6

CHAPTER 2
The British plan and available strengths
18

CHAPTER 3
9 April 1917 on the Third Army's front
38

CHAPTER 4
The Canadian offensive at Vimy
58

CHAPTER 5
The impossible breakthrough
80

CHAPTER 6
The Australians in Bullecourt and the end of the British offensive
90

CHAPTER 7
The French plan and general Nivelle's forces
102

CHAPTER 8
The German army on alert
116

CHAPTER 9
The offensive on the front of the 6e armée
128

CHAPITRE 10
16 April 1917 on the front of the 5e armée
142

CHAPTER 11
The battle in the following days
160

CHAPTER 12
The offensive continues
174

BIBLIOGRAPHY

R.G. NOBÉCOURT - *Les fantassins du Chemin des Dames*
Editions Bertout, Luneray, 1983

D. PORRET - *Les As français de la Grande Guerre*
SHAA, Vincennes, 1983. Two volumes

SHAT - *Les armées françaises dans la Grande Guerre*
Tome V, part one and tome VI part one,
Annexes 1 et 2. Paris, Imprimerie nationale, 1931

AEF - *Histories of 251 divisions of the German Army*
which participated in the war
London, Stamp Exchange, 1989

JEAN DE PIERREFEU - *GQG secteur 1*
Paris, L'Edition Française illustrée, 1920. Part one

GUY PÉDRONCINI - *Les mutineries de 1917*
PUF, Paris, 1983

GUY PÉDRONCINI - *Journal de guerre de Joffre*
SHAT, Vincennes, 1990

ERICH LUDENDORFF - *Souvenirs de guerre*
Payot, Paris, 1920. Part two

DOUGLAS HAIG - *Carnets secrets*
Presses de la Cité, Paris, 1964

J.C. DUNN - *The War the infantry knew*
Cardinal, London, 1991

SHAT - *Les troupes coloniales pendant la Grande Guerre*
Paris, Imprimerie nationale, 1931

J.H. JOHNSON - *Stalemate*
Arms & Armour Press, London, 1995

SIEGFRIED SASSOON - *Memoirs of an Infantry Officer*
Faber & Faber, London, 1982

SIEGFRIED SASSOON - *Siegfried's Journey*
Faber & Faber, London, 1982

CEW BEAN - *The Australian Imperial Force in France 1917*
Volume IV. University of Queensland Press, 1982

GEORGES GAUDY - *Le Chemin des Dames en feu*
Paris, Plon, 1921

JEAN NORTON CRU - *Témoins*
PUN, Nancy, 1994

ROBERT GRAVES - *Goodbye to All That*
Penguin, London, 1979

EDMUND BLUNDEN - *Undertones of War*
Penguin, London, 1982

RENÉ NAEGELEN - *Les suppliciés, histoire vécue*
Baudinière, Paris, 1927

PIERRE WALINE - *Les Crapouillots*
Charles Lavauzelle, Paris

J. TEZENAS DU MONTCEL - *L'Heure H. Etapes d'infanterie*
SNEV, Paris, 1960

RAYMOND PELLOUTIER - *La voix d'un Jeune*
Figuière, Paris, 1930

G. LEROY - *Pacifiques combattants*
Marcel Leconte, Marseille, 1935

DUCASSE, MEYER ET PERREUX - *Vie et Mort des Français 1914-18*
Hachette, Paris

The author wishes to thank all those who helped him while compiling this work, particularly the following:

Pierrette Blondlet *(BDIC)*
Philippe Charbonnier
Frau Hoffman *(Bundesarchiv)*
Jean-Marie Mongin
Philippe Teulé
François Vauvillier

Publishing Manager : Patrick Rivière
Design : FABECO
Translated by Bernard Leprêtre

ISBN : 2 908 182 66 1
Publisher's number : 2 908 182
Published by,
Histoire & Collections
5, avenue de la République
75011 Paris - France
Tél. international 01 40 21 18 20
Fax. international 01 47 00 51 11

Editorial composition :
Power Pc 8500, logiciels
Quark X Press, Adobe Photoshop.

Colour separation : Arrigo
Printed by Hérissey on
30 th March 1997